UNBELIEVABLE FOOTBALL 2

For Arlo, my favourite game-changer

First published in Great Britain in 2021 by Wren & Rook

ISBN: 978 1526 36553 8
E-book ISBN: 978 1526 36422 7

10 9 8 7 6 5 4 3 2 1

MIX
Paper from responsible sources
FSC® C104740

Wren & Rook
An imprint of
Hachette Children's Group
Part of Hodder & Stoughton
Carmelite House
50 Victoria Embankment
London EC4Y 0DZ

An Hachette UK Company
www.hachette.co.uk
www.hachettechildrens.co.uk

Editorial Director: Laura Horsley
Art Director: Laura Hambleton
Designed by Clare Mills

Printed in the United Kingdom

UNBELIEVABLE FOOTBALL 2

WRITTEN BY
MATT OLDFIELD

ILLUSTRATIONS BY
OLLIE MANN

wren & rook

CONTENTS

INTRODUCTION

Introduction

Hello there, ready to read more unbelievable stories from the fascinating world of football? If so, well done, you've opened the right book! Perhaps you've picked this up because you enjoyed the first one, or perhaps you love football and the word is in the title, or perhaps you were wowed by the incredible, colourful cover (great work, Ollie Mann!) and saw Marcus Rashford's smiling face. Whatever your reason, welcome to the *Unbelievable Football* club.

While we come from different places, have different ages (no, I'm not telling you how old I am!) and play with different levels of skill, we members are all united by one key fact: we really love football. Why? Well, for lots of reasons, but in this book, I'll be focusing on one in particular: not only is football the most popular sport on the planet, but it's also the most powerful.

'Wait, what do you mean by "powerful"?' I hear some of you asking. 'Does football have the strength of Superman, the brains of Batman and the speed of Spider-Man?'

No, not exactly, but think about how much football means to you – add up all the time you spend playing it, watching it, talking about it, thinking about it, dreaming about it each and every day. Approximately 24 hours, right? And if it can have that much impact on your life, imagine what it could have on the whole wide world! That's why football is the most powerful sport on the planet and, in this book, you'll learn about lots of different, unbelievable ways in which the game we love has helped to change the world and make it a better place.

There's **'Football(ers) for Change'**, a collection of tales about individual players (and one famous fan) who have fought for important progress both on and off the pitch, and **'Amazing Acts of Kindness'**, where you'll learn about how generous footballers can be. **'Football United'** is a section of stories about how teams have brought peace to countries in conflict, and in **'Protecting the Planet'**, you'll learn about how 'green' they can be too. **'Football for a Brighter Future'** focuses on awesome organisations that are inspiring the next generation to get involved, and finally, there's **'Incredible Kids'**, a collection of stories showcasing the passion and compassion of young people around the world.

Plus, as if that's not enough unbelievable content for one unbelievable book, you'll also discover how you can play your part and follow in the footsteps of your new football heroes.

Sound good? Well, get comfortable and get ready to change the world through football!

CHAPTER ONE

FOOTBALL(ERS) FOR CHANGE

Marvellous Marcus Rashford and the Fight to End Food Poverty

Being a famous footballer definitely has its ups and downs. Yes, the money is really good and there's lots of glory up for grabs, but life in the public eye comes with a lot of extra pressures. All's well when you're playing well; when you're not, though, your millions of fans and followers will certainly let you know about it:

'You're rubbish – our club should get rid of you!'

So, it takes a very brave and special footballer to use social media to stand up, speak out and fight for social change. That's exactly what Manchester United and England forward **Marcus Rashford** did in March 2020 when the COVID-19 crisis led to a national lockdown. Since scoring a double on his United debut in 2016 at the age of only 18, Rashford has gone on to become a superstar for club and country, but he hasn't forgotten where he came from. So, when he heard the news that

all schools would have to close, his first concern was: 'What about the vulnerable kids – what are they going to eat now?'

Rashford thought back to his own childhood experiences in Wythenshawe, Manchester, when his mum, Melanie, had worked three different jobs in order to put food on the table for her young family each night. Marcus's favourite meal is still the same – chicken and rice, made by his mum! Yum. But that was only dinner; for the other two meals of the day, young Marcus had relied on the breakfast club and free school lunches at Button Lane Primary. So, what would have happened to him during the COVID-19 crisis? Well, he would have gone hungry, and without the energy and concentration that food provided, he might not have gone on to become a top footballer. Imagine that, Manchester United and England fans!

Marcus worried that the government might not do enough to feed the 1.4 million kids across England who were allowed free school meals, and so he was determined to do something to help stop them from going hungry. But what? His first step was to contact a food charity called FareShare to make a big donation to help children in the Manchester area. However, the more he learned about the organisation and the work they did to distribute meals to families in need, the more Marcus wanted to get fully involved in tackling food poverty. As well as money, he could also offer his time and effort, especially while he recovered from a back injury. And most importantly of all, he could use his powerful voice to reach out and spread the message to his millions of followers on Instagram and Twitter.

'WHEN YOU GET TO THE POSITION I'M IN NOW, I FEEL LIKE IF CHILDREN ARE IN NEED, AND THEY DON'T HAVE ANYONE FIGHTING FOR THEM, I SHOULD BE THE ONE THAT DOES IT REALLY. '

When Rashford first started tweeting about free school meals and his work with FareShare, many fans told him to focus on football and leave politics alone. But luckily, Rashford didn't listen. Why couldn't he be a gamechanger both on and off the pitch? He was determined to use his platform as a famous footballer for good. So, he carried on speaking out, from the heart and from experience. Go on, Marcus!

With Rashford's help, FareShare soon reached their target of £20 million, which meant they could provide much-needed meals for millions more children across the country. Although that was brilliant news, it was only a short-term fix and it wasn't enough. Lots of people had lost their jobs during the COVID-19 crisis, which meant they couldn't afford to feed their families. More people than ever had no choice but to visit food banks instead, just like Rashford himself had as a kid. Sadly, the food poverty problem in England wasn't getting any better.

Big social changes were needed, but how could Rashford get the government to listen? When they cancelled their food voucher scheme over the summer holiday, he decided that it was time for him to go further and take proper political action. So, in June 2020, Rashford wrote a personal letter to MPs in Parliament, saying:

> **THIS IS ENGLAND IN 2020, AND THIS IS AN ISSUE THAT NEEDS URGENT ASSISTANCE. PLEASE, WHILE THE EYES OF THE NATION ARE ON YOU, MAKE THE U-TURN AND MAKE PROTECTING THE LIVES OF SOME OF OUR MOST VULNERABLE A TOP PRIORITY.**
> **YOURS SINCERELY,**
> **MARCUS RASHFORD**

And it worked. Just one day and thousands of likes and retweets later, the Prime Minister Boris Johnson changed his mind and announced that he was extending free school meals for children during the summer holidays. Hurray, what a win for team #ENDCHILDFOODPOVERTY! As the scoreline on one proud banner in Wythenshawe read, it was:

'RASHFORD 1, BORIS 0.'

Although he was really proud of the part he had played so far, Rashford didn't stop there. As all you football fans will know, 1–0 is a nerve-wracking scoreline to defend, so on 1 September 2020, he went on the attack again. He created a new Child Food Poverty Task Force, which included all the major supermarkets, plus lots of food businesses and charities. The hope was that by working together, just like Rashford and his United teammates on the football pitch, the task force could find a long-term solution to the child food poverty problem.

However, as the October half-term approached, Rashford returned to the same old short-term issue –

how were the kids going to eat? You see, the government had extended their voucher scheme over the summer, but not for all school holidays. FareShare would do their best to deliver as many meals as possible, but it wouldn't be enough to feed everyone. So, once again, Rashford got political, posting an online petition called 'End child food poverty – no child should be going hungry'.

In the UK, if 100,000 people sign a petition, then the government has to discuss it in Parliament. Well, thanks to the power of social media, Rashford's petition reached that figure within ten hours and the number kept on rising! Surely, the subject of free school meals needed to be discussed immediately, in time for half-term? But no, the idea of an early debate was rejected by MPs. Boooo!

Well, if the government wouldn't help the hungry at half-term, then it was up to kind citizens across the country. Just like the local chip shop that used to slip young Marcus bags of chips, hundreds of cafés and restaurants agreed to hand out free meals to families in need, and Rashford shared the details on social media.

It was an amazing moment of unity in such troubled times; in the middle of the COVID-19 crisis, which had taken so many lives and jobs, the people of England had come together to help each other, inspired by a brave and tireless campaign from one of their most famous footballers.

We love you Marcus, we do!

Yes, he was the new number one national hero, no matter which team you supported, or whether you even liked sport at all. Some people were even saying that he should become the next Prime Minister! And just in case anyone still thought Rashford should focus only on football, he showed that his fight for social change wasn't affecting his performances on the pitch at all. If anything, he was better than ever. On the same day that his petition passed a million signatures, he scored a phenomenal hat-trick as a Manchester United super sub in the Champions League against RB Leipzig.

'3 goals, 16 minutes, 1,030,000 signatures. Can't stop smiling,' he tweeted after the game.

Rashford was on a roll, and no one could stop him, not even the government. At last, on 8 November, he received a response about his petition from the Prime Minister himself. Over the next 12 months, the government would spend more than £400 million to support poor children and their families in England. Hurray, another wonderful win for team #ENDCHILDFOODPOVERTY!

But Rashford didn't rest, not when there was still so much more to be done. At Christmas, he teamed up with former Manchester United manager Sir Alex Ferguson and *The Times* newspaper for a special campaign, which raised a further £3 million for FareShare. The extra money meant more meals and the charity was also able to open a new warehouse. They asked Marcus to name it, and what did he call it? Melanie Maynard House, in honour of his hard-working mum who had done so much to help him become a top footballer *and* a top human being.

What a hero! And Rashford isn't the only famous footballer who's fighting to end food poverty. Chelsea and England right-back **Reece James** has been working closely with a London charity called The Felix Project. As well as raising lots of money and awareness, he has also served meals to struggling local families, and even delivered food parcels to homeless shelters on Christmas Eve. 'I've got the opportunity and the power to help,' James explained. 'I think helping others is not going to harm me, it's only going to benefit other people.'

So, the next time you hear someone moan that 'all modern footballers are selfish, stupid and overpaid', remember the good guys like Rashford and James, players who are using their privileged position and platform to fight for positive change in the world. And winning. Hurray!

'I DON'T HAVE THE EDUCATION OF A POLITICIAN, MANY ON TWITTER HAVE MADE THAT CLEAR TODAY, BUT I HAVE A SOCIAL EDUCATION HAVING LIVED THROUGH THIS AND HAVING SPENT TIME WITH THE FAMILIES AND CHILDREN MOST AFFECTED. THESE CHILDREN MATTER. THESE CHILDREN ARE THE FUTURE OF THIS COUNTRY. THEY ARE NOT JUST ANOTHER STATISTIC. AND FOR AS LONG AS THEY DON'T HAVE A VOICE, THEY WILL HAVE MINE.'

– Marcus Rashford

SPEAKING UP!

Marcus Rashford isn't the only famous footballer using social media to campaign for social change. His England teammate **Raheem Sterling** has become one of the modern leaders in the fight to kick racism out of football. After years of suffering discrimination due to the colour of his skin, on 8 December 2018, Sterling finally decided enough was enough. 'I am not normally the person to talk a lot but when I think I need my point heard I will speak up,' he posted on Instagram.

The previous night, Sterling had been playing a match for Manchester City, when he went over to the touchline to get the ball and take a corner-kick for his team. Usually, he was so focused on football that he didn't even notice the fans around him, but on this particular day, they were impossible to ignore. A few of the opposition supporters in the front row of the stand were so close that Raheem could have reached out and touched them, and some of them were angrily shouting racist insults right into his face.

Can you even begin to imagine how horrible that would be? The incident left Sterling feeling sad and frustrated, but not surprised. Unfortunately, he had experienced racism many times before – during his childhood days in Wembley after leaving Jamaica at the age of two, and also later during his early years as a player at QPR and Liverpool. But it was too much now. He refused to keep quiet any longer. The abuse was totally unacceptable, and as one of the world's most famous footballers, he was in a powerful position to do something about it. He wanted to give hope to the next generation of young black kids, to inspire them to see that, like him, they could fight discrimination and do whatever they wanted to do.

So, the next day, Sterling decided to speak up and show that racism wasn't just a problem in football stadiums, but in society as a whole. How was the situation supposed to get better when players still weren't being treated equally in the media? To prove it, he posted pictures of newspaper articles about two of his young Manchester City teammates, one black (Tosin Adarabioyo) and one white (Phil Foden). Both players had done the same thing – buy an expensive house for their mothers to say thank you for all their support – but spot the difference between these headlines:

'Young Manchester City footballer, 20, on £25,000 a week splashes out on mansion on market for £2.25 million despite having never started a Premier League match.'

'Manchester City starlet Phil Foden buys new £2m home for his mum.'

The same story told in two very different ways – flashy young kid versus kind family man. What do you think when you see those headlines? It doesn't seem fair, does it? And it could be dangerous too. When newspapers publish articles, millions read them, and they can have a big impact on how people think and behave. That's why Sterling was sending out a message: 'for all newspapers that don't understand why people are racist in this day and age all I have to say is have a second thought about fair publicity and give all players an equal chance.'

It's now over 130 years since Arthur Wharton became the first black footballer to play in the English Football League, and yet there are still players being discriminated against because of the colour of their skin. It's not OK, and it has to stop. You'll probably have seen Premier League players wearing the 'No Room for Racism' badge on their shirts and taking the knee together before kick-off, but Tyrone Mings, Tammy Abraham, Wilfried Zaha, Axel Tuanzebe and Trent Alexander-Arnold are just a few of the many black players who have recently received totally unacceptable abuse, both online and on the pitch. As Sterling puts it, 'The racism problem in football is so bad, runs so deep and is nowhere near being sorted.'

And it's not just an English problem. During a Spanish league match in 2020, Athletic Bilbao's **Iñaki Williams** was the subject of racist chants from a rival team's supporters. The forward reported the incident to the referee, and then used Twitter to talk to the world: 'It's really sad that today we carry on living with these racist moments in football. We have to stop it.' In Italy, Inter Milan striker **Romelu**

Lukaku has also used social media to speak out against the racism he has experienced: 'Football is a game to be enjoyed by everyone and we shouldn't accept any form of discrimination that will put our game in shame.'

So, what part can we football fans play in achieving equality and ending discrimination? Well, we have to stand together, united against racism, treating everyone as equals – both our teammates and our opponents. Like Sterling, Williams and Lukaku, we must speak up against racism whenever and wherever we hear it – whether in a stadium or on the pitch, at school or in the street. If the discrimination is directed at you, don't be afraid to talk about it and get the support you need from friends, family, teachers and coaches. And if the abuse is aimed at someone else instead, try to be the best ally you can be, just like **Pat Nevin** back in 1984.

It was 14 April, and Nevin's club Chelsea were playing Crystal Palace away at Selhurst Park. The first-half of the match was so boring that I won't even bother to talk about it. Instead, let's fast forward to the 62nd minute when the

Chelsea manager John Neal decided to make an attacking substitution and bring on **Paul Canoville**, an exciting young forward and the first black player ever to play for the club.

Actually, the next 20 minutes of football were pretty terrible too, so let's fast forward again to the 83rd minute when Canoville, the super sub, set up Nevin to score the only goal of the game. Another win for Chelsea! When the final whistle blew, it should have been a time for celebrations, but their 'wee' (that's Scottish for small, by the way) wing wizard didn't see it that way. Nevin's joy at scoring the winner had been replaced by anger at the racism he had heard from some of his own fans, and which was aimed at one of their own players.

Yes, Canoville had been booed and abused by some Chelsea supporters from the moment he made his debut back in 1982: 'It should have been one of the greatest days of my life, not a nightmare that came back again and again.' Two years later, some supporters were still shouting the same totally unacceptable things at Canoville. Why? Sadly, it was because of the colour of his skin.

There were more and more brilliant black players in English football – John Barnes at Watford, West Brom's 'The Three Degrees' Cyrille Regis, Laurie Cunningham and Brendon Batson, plus Nottingham Forest defender Viv Anderson, who in 1978 had become the first black player to represent England in an international match. Despite their success, these footballers still suffered horrendous abuse, even from their own so-called 'fans'. And when it happened to them, the players were often told to just keep quiet and carry on, which only made the problem worse. As Canoville's shocking story shows, black footballers faced a constant battle to survive:

'I remember scoring a goal and hearing that some fans wouldn't have it because a black player scored. It didn't count, so they said we had lost not drawn. How do you live like that? I had to control my anger so many times so outsiders couldn't see. I had to see the bigger picture.'

Something had to be done to stop the racism in English football, and so after that match at Crystal Palace, Nevin spoke out in support of his teammate, Canoville. He couldn't ignore the horrible discrimination any longer. The TV presenter tried to ask him about his winning goal, but the Chelsea star wanted to talk about something far more important.

'I'm disgusted by the fans,' Nevin announced. 'How dare they boo any Chelsea player and to do it because he is black is sickening.'

No, Pat's post-match interview didn't put an end to all racism in English football, but his powerful words were heard on TV screens all over the country and they did make a difference. The Chelsea fans listened to their star player and thought about their awful actions. At their next home match, rather than booing and abusing Canoville, the supporters sang his name. It was a small but significant step in the right direction.

'I respected Pat and was honoured when he came out and said what he said,' Canoville said. 'I was getting hardcore abuse. But he scored, and he made that statement and boy did people take notice. It eased things for me.'

It's up to each and every one of us to fight for what is

right, with our actions as well as our words. So, what would you do if, like Nevin, you heard discrimination directed at one of your teammates? In a recent Spanish league game, the whole Valencia team left the field in protest when one of their players suffered alleged racist abuse. And in a Champions League match in February 2021 between French club PSG and Turkish club İstanbul Başakşehir, both teams agreed to walk off the pitch. Together, we're stronger, and we can help make football a more beautiful game and the world a better place.

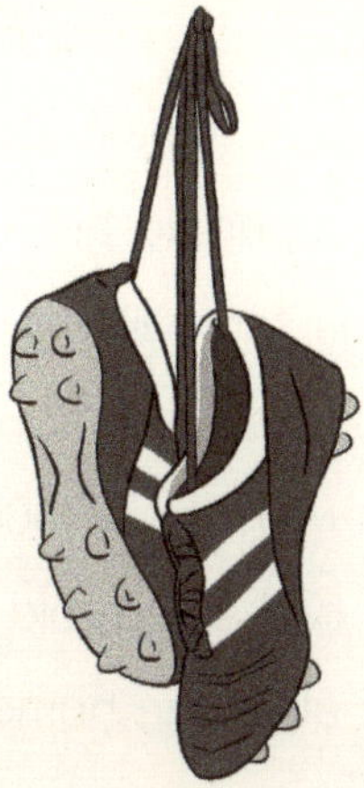

The Skilful Scot Who Kicked Down Barriers

From one fearless Scot to another – meet **Rose Reilly**, a pioneering superstar who battled past barriers and discrimination to become the only Scot ever to win the World Cup. So far!

Reilly lifted the trophy – the Mundialito as it was known at the time, meaning 'Little World Cup' – in 1984, but she did it wearing the bright blue of Italy rather than the navy blue of her homeland. 'Why Italy?' you might be wondering. Because, as a female, that was where Reilly had to go in order to pursue her childhood dream of becoming a professional footballer.

Reilly grew up in a town called Stewarton, about 20 miles south of Glasgow, in the 1960s. At the time, a lot of people in Scotland had a very old-fashioned view of a woman's role: to look after the home and raise children. So, young girls were expected to like dolls, tea parties and dresses, but not Rose. No, even at the age of four, she was already breaking the rules. When she was given a doll as a Christmas present, she swapped it for the thing she had always wanted: a football.

Rose slept with the ball in her bed, partly because she loved it so much, and partly because she was worried that her mother would take it away. Professional women's football had been banned in Britain since 1921 because it was seen as 'quite unsuitable for females', so her parents didn't see the point in her playing. Why couldn't she focus on another sport instead, like athletics or tennis? Because football is way more fun, duh! (No offence, Usain Bolt and Serena Williams.)

Rose had fallen in love with football, and nothing was going to stop her – not the disapproval of her parents, and not the daily tellings-off from her teachers at school. She was born to play the beautiful game; she just needed to find a way to become a superstar …

When she was seven, the local boys' club, Stewarton Boys, invited her to join, but only on two conditions:

1) she cut her hair short

and

2) she changed her name to Ross

'No problem!' Rose replied and off she raced to the barbers. She was willing to do anything in order to play football. Straight away, 'Ross' became the star of the Stewarton Boys team. With her speed, strength, passion and skill, no defence could stop her from scoring. She was so good that a scout from the top Scottish club Celtic (Rose's favourite team) asked about signing their sensational number 7, until the coach told him the truth:

'Sorry, she's a girl!'

'Why does that make any difference?' young Rose tried to argue. Surely, a good footballer was a good footballer, whether lad or lassie (that's Scottish for girl, by the way)? But it was no use; as fun as it was to play with the boys, it was clear that she would never be fully accepted. So, 'Ross' went back to being Rose and became a star striker for Stewarton Thistle Ladies instead. She made her debut for their senior women's team in 1965 at the age of only

ten – talk about a wonderkid, eh!

By playing against fully grown adults, Rose got better and better. In 1971, she led her club all the way to the first-ever Women's FA Cup final and, a year later, she was picked to play for her country in Scotland's first women's international match against England. She had achieved all that by the age of 17, so what else was there to aim for?

Sadly, it seemed that if Rose wanted to progress and become a professional, she would have to move away from home. In 1971, when UEFA held a vote on whether to include and promote women's football within national organisations, 31 of the 32 countries said yes. The one that said no? Scotland.

Rose was disappointed in her country, but she was too determined to let one stupid, wrong decision stop her. Football was her life, all she had ever wanted to do, and so she wasn't going to give up now. For years, she had been dreaming about playing for a team in Europe, so why not turn it into a reality? When she spoke to a Scottish sportswriter about her plan, he told her about an Irish footballer called Anna O'Brien who had recently signed for a team in France called Stade de Reims.

'Sounds perfect!' Rose said, and so she set off with two of her talented Scottish teammates, Edna Neillis and Elsie Cook, to take part in a trial match. Reims were so impressed that they signed all three of them at half-time!

For Rose, that was the start of an amazing, 23-year European adventure. After six months in France, she moved to Italy because AC Milan made her an offer she couldn't refuse – the chance to play football in the most professional women's league around, and score goals at the San Siro Stadium, in front of up to 80,000 supporters!

Milan and Stewarton were two totally different worlds – as she says herself, 'I hadn't even eaten spaghetti hoops before I went there, never mind the real spaghetti!' – but Rose was determined to make the most of her opportunity. She loved the Italian culture and quickly learned the language, plus, thanks to all her hard work in training, she soon found her top form on the pitch. During her four years at the club, she won two league titles and became one of the biggest stars in Italian football. One club, Lecce, were so desperate to sign her that they put in a brand-new grass pitch just to please her! In total, Rose played for nine clubs in Italy, winning eight league titles, four Italian Cups and two Serie A Golden Boot awards (for most goals scored).

And that was only one part of her incredible trophy cabinet. In 1980, Rose pulled off the impressive trick of winning two league titles in two different countries in one season! On Saturdays, she starred for Lecce in Italy, and then on Sundays, she flew to France to star for her old club, Reims. Amazing, and modern footballers complain about playing two matches in a week ...

As much as she loved her new double life in Italy and France, Rose hadn't forgotten about her homeland. She wanted to carry on playing for her country, but the Scottish Women's FA wouldn't let her. In fact, they decided to ban her for life. Why? Because she had dared to go abroad to chase her football dream and become a better player.

That was so unfair, but Rose didn't let it get her down for long. If Scotland didn't want her any more, then she would just star for Italy instead. It turned out to be a brilliant decision because she was picked to play at the 1984 Women's World Cup and led her second nation all the way to the final.

Ahead of the big game against West Germany, Rose and her teammates stood together for the national anthem, and instead of 'Brothers of Italy', they sang 'Sisters of Italy'. It was a really powerful moment for women's football and the fight for equal opportunities. Why shouldn't everyone be allowed to play the sport they love? Although Scotland had let her down, Rose had found another way to achieve her dream.

And she had also saved her best performance for the World Cup final. First, Rose set up her strike partner, Carolina Morace, with a perfect cross from the left, and then she scored Italy's second goal herself. After helping the team to grab a third, the manager decided to take her off, but the fans weren't happy. They booed because they wanted to see more of the best player on the planet!

Yes, Rose had reached the very top of women's football. Not only was she now a World Cup winner, but she was also the Female World Footballer of the Year. Through hard work, courage and incredible determination, the talented young striker from Stewarton had achieved her professional football dream, plus a whole lot more.

So, were the Scottish people proud of their World Cup winner? It took another 20 years, but at last, Rose is now getting the recognition she deserves in her homeland. In

2007, she became one of only 50 players to enter the Scottish Football Hall of Fame, and the first-ever female. And in 2020, Rose also received an MBE for her services to women's football – all over the world, but especially in Scotland. Her remarkable story and achievements have helped to inspire an exciting new generation of footballers, including Kim Little, Caroline Weir and Erin Cuthbert, who in 2019, helped Scotland qualify for the Women's World Cup for the first time. Yes, thanks to rebellious Rose, the future of women's football in Scotland now looks brighter than ever.

'WHEN I WAS A WEE GIRL OF SEVEN, THIS WAS MY DREAM – TO PLAY PROFESSIONAL FOOTBALL – AND I MADE IT COME TRUE!'

'IF YOU WANT SOMETHING IN LIFE, JUST GO FOR IT. NEVER EVER LET ANYBODY SAY NO TO YOU.'

Equal Pay to Play: The Team Protest that Went Viral

Despite the brave acts of stars like Rose Reilly, the fight for equality goes on in our beautiful game. In order to change the world, we must continue to stand up, speak out and take action, just like the **Cyprus women's national football team** did in 2019.

Cyprus is a European island in the Mediterranean Sea, and sits just south of Turkey. It's famous for its delicious food (kebabs and halloumi, anyone?), sunny weather and ancient buildings, but not for its football talent (no offence!). Have you ever heard of Nikodimos Papavasiliou? No, I didn't think so, and neither had I until recently. Papavasiliou signed for Newcastle United in 1993, becoming the first Cypriot ever to play in the Premier League. Sadly, seven games and zero goals later, the midfielder moved on to Greece.

So no, football has not been a success story for Cyprus.

The men's national team was formed in 1949, and since then, they have failed to qualify for a single World Cup or European Championship. And the women's team? Well, their record was even worse, but that wasn't their fault. They had only played their first official international match in 2002, and then, for the next 17 years, the Cypriot Football Federation refused to register them for any World Cup or European Championship. The women's team weren't even given their own kits; instead, they had to borrow from the male youth teams. With no respect and nothing to play for, lots of the country's top female players quit the team until, eventually, the federation agreed to enter them for the UEFA Women's Euro 2021.

Progress at last! The Cyprus women's national football team were pleased, but they didn't stop there. Now that they had achieved their first aim – equal opportunities to play – they moved on to their next – equal pay. Cyprus's female footballers were not professional players, so for every international match they had to take time off from their day jobs. And what did the football federation pay them while they were away? Just €20 per day! That was nowhere near enough, especially compared to what the men's team earned. But why shouldn't the women receive the same amount of money for doing the same job? And why shouldn't they have access to the same training facilities and equipment?

In November 2019, those questions were still unanswered as the Cyprus women's national team set off for their second Euro 2021 qualifier against Finland. It turned out to be a very significant match because as well as being a top team, Finland were also leading the fight for football change. Just two months earlier, the Finnish FA had announced that their women's national team would be paid the same as their men's team. 'We want to be involved in the development of a more responsible and equal society,' the chairman Ari Lahti had said.

The Cyprus women's national team shared the same goal, and the trip to Finland inspired them to take action too. Before kick-off, they gathered together in the dressing room to pose for a team photo with a difference: every player had a blue equality sign painted on their hand (the equals symbol you use in Maths). It was a really powerful image of strength and solidarity, which they then shared with the world through social media.

'ATHLETES SHOULD NOT BE AFRAID TO CLAIM EQUALITY.'

– Maria Ioannou, player for the Cyprus women's national football team

When they saw the photo, the Cyprus football federation were furious. They tried to silence their players by threatening to drop them from the team, but it was too late – their political act had already got people talking. The campaign went viral, with thousands of people showing their support by sharing pictures of their painted equality signs. The Cyprus Footballers' Association, the men's national team and most of the country were standing up with them, side by side. So, rather than back down and say sorry, the Cyprus women's team stayed strong and kept protesting. In March 2020, the players announced that they would refuse to play any more international matches unless the football federation agreed to meet with them to discuss equal pay.

In the end, Cyprus finished bottom of their Euro 2021 qualifying group with zero points and zero goals, but their players were able to celebrate a different kind of victory. Their courage and determination had helped kick off a new conversation between the Cyprus Footballers' Association and the Cypriot Parliament about gender equality in sports. There's still a long way to go – and sadly COVID-19 has slowed down the discussions – but at least the country is finally taking steps in the right direction.

Meanwhile, the media attention isn't going away – the Cyprus team won one of the 2020 FIFPRO Merit Awards alongside Marcus Rashford – and neither is the players' passion for the fight for equality. One of their stars, Filippa Savva, now plays in England for Lewes FC, the first football club in the world to pay their women's team the same wages as their men's team.

Progress at last! Yes, country by country, women footballers across the world are winning the fight for equal pay. Finland, Australia, Norway and New Zealand were the ones who led the way, with the likes of England and Brazil following in 2020. But amazingly, the battle still goes on in the USA, where the WNT (women's national soccer team) are four-time World Champions, while the men's team are still stuck on ... zero. As Americans like to say, 'Go figure!' WNT stars Megan Rapinoe and Margaret 'Midge' Purce did meet with President Joe Biden at a recent 'Equal Pay Day' event at the White House, though, so watch this space ...

Mahatma Gandhi's Passive Resisters

As you've just read, famous footballers sometimes make amazing political activists, but did you also know that famous political activists are sometimes big football fans? Yes, you might know **Mohandas 'Mahatma' Gandhi** as the sandal-wearing lawyer who used non-violent protest to fight for India's freedom, but let me take you back to his younger years in England and South Africa, when he first developed his passion for sport.

In 1893, Gandhi, aged 23, arrived in the South African city of Durban to start work as a lawyer, after completing his years of study at University College, London. However, despite his education and qualifications, he found that that he was treated differently. Why? Sadly, because of the colour of his skin. The white South African government had introduced a racist policy called segregation (later, after 1950, it would become known as 'apartheid'), which meant that people from other races were not allowed to live, or own businesses or land, in certain areas of the country. Black Africans were also forced to use separate bathrooms, restaurants and shops, as well as sit in separate sections on public transport.

Gandhi was Asian and faced the same discrimination as the black community. On a train journey from Durban to Pretoria, he was told he had to leave the first-class carriage, despite having a first-class ticket. Why? Because the law said that only white people were allowed to sit there. When Gandhi stood his ground and tried to argue his case, they threw him off the train altogether.

Gandhi was so disgusted by the racism he and others around him experienced that he was determined to do something about it. But what could he do to make a difference? He didn't believe that violence was the right way to fight for social change so, instead, he would use peaceful protest and resistance.

'IN A GENTLE WAY, YOU CAN SHAKE THE WORLD.'

– Mahatma Ghandi

He called this idea 'Satyagraha', which means 'holding firmly to truth' in Sanskrit. Gandhi formed a new political group called the Natal Indian Congress to peacefully fight discrimination against Indians in South Africa. He also led a campaign for all non-whites in the country to have the right to vote too. However, the more active Gandhi became in South African politics, the angrier some local people became. In 1897, he was viciously attacked by a group of young white men as he arrived in Durban by boat, but that didn't stop him; in fact, it spurred him on to think bigger. In order to spread his political message far and wide, Gandhi was going to need to find a great way to reach out and bring lots of people together to listen.

And that's where football came in. It was during his days in England that Gandhi had first noticed the power of the game, and the passion that it inspired in people. Through the London Vegetarian Society, he had become friends with a man called Arnold Hills, a keen sportsman who would go on to found Thames Ironworks Football Club, now known as West Ham United FC!

In Gandhi's new home, South Africa, while the white people preferred to play rugby and cricket, football was the favourite sport of the black population. Large crowds of people turned up to watch the very popular local matches.

'Perfect!' Gandhi thought, about his clever plan to combine football with politics. He had already helped to form the Transvaal Indian Football Association in 1896, the first organised football group in Africa that wasn't run by white people. Then, he took things a step further, by creating his own football club that would join the peaceful fight for equal rights.

The first Passive Resisters Soccer Club was formed in Durban, and Gandhi formed another two with the same name in the South African cities of Pretoria and Johannesburg. Sadly, there's no evidence of the great man himself ever pulling on the black-and-white shirt and playing on the pitch, but there are certainly photos of him at the matches, cheering his team on. And with a large crowd there watching, Gandhi often took the opportunity to hand out his political leaflets and make speeches about non-violent resistance either after the final whistle or at half-time. It was all a little more serious than the crossbar challenges and mascot races you find at most modern football matches! Plus, any money raised at the matches was donated to the families of those who had been jailed for non-violent resistance.

Meanwhile, out on the football pitch, Gandhi saw the beautiful game as a great way to promote key ideas like teamwork and fair play, which are just as important in politics and society as they are in sport. Only by working together as a united group would the black, mixed-race and Asian South Africans stand a chance of fighting the discrimination they faced.

In 1915, Gandhi returned to India to begin another fight, this time for his country's independence from the British Empire. But what about his political football project in South Africa? Well, sadly the Passive Resisters struggled without their founder and, by 1936, all three teams had stopped playing. However, Gandhi had also inspired other clubs, including one called Christopher's Contingent, which became the first South African football team to go on an international tour, in 1921. And where did they go? To India, with a little assistance from Gandhi and his friends, who helped to organise the trip and their opponents!

Unfortunately, the fight for racial equality in South Africa had to continue for a very long time, both in society and in sport. It was only in the early 1990s, over 75 years after Gandhi had left the country, that future President of South Africa Nelson Mandela and other peacemakers finally managed to put an end to the awful apartheid system. In 1991, a new multi-racial South African Football Association was formed, and FIFA finally allowed the national team to play in their competitions again, after a 15-year ban due to apartheid.

Just five years later, the 'Bafana Bafana' (another awesome nickname!) entered their first-ever African Cup of Nations and won it, beating Tunisia 2–0 in the final. It was an amazing sporting triumph for South Africa, but the team itself was just as important as the trophy. As a beautiful symbol of the new 'Rainbow Nation', their line-up featured white and black South Africans playing side by side. Mark Fish partnered Lucas Radebe in central defence, with Eric Tinkler racing up the right wing and John 'Shoes' Moshoeu skilling his way up the left.

Almost 100 years after Gandhi had first used football to begin the fight for social change, now, at last, a new, united South Africa was emerging, both on and off the pitch.

And just in case you still weren't sure about the link between Gandhi and football, there's even a Brazilian midfielder called Mahatma Gandhi Heberpio Mattos Pires, or 'Mahatma' for short. Sadly, he doesn't really take after his non-violent namesake. In a league match in 2013, Mahatma picked up two yellow cards in just ten minutes and was sent off!

Sam Weller Widdowson – An All-Round Sporting Genius

So far in this section, you've heard four inspiring stories of football heroes who have used their fame and influence to fight for change in the wider world. But I'd like to finish by telling you about a very clever Victorian who instead changed the game of football itself.

Sam Weller Widdowson was a man of many sporting talents. As well as playing cricket for Nottinghamshire, he was also an excellent runner and hurdler, who somehow found the time to play football for Nottingham Forest and England too. In fact, he was part of the national team that travelled to Scotland in 1880, for one of the very first international matches. On the teamsheet, Widdowson is listed as a 'forward', although there were quite a few of them that day, as England went for a very attacking 2-2-6 formation. Perhaps that's why they lost 4–5!

As if all that wasn't enough, Widdowson was also a man of many new sporting ideas. When Nottingham Forest made him captain in 1873, he quickly changed the team's formation to 2-3-5 (still a bit too attacking if you ask me!), which proved very popular throughout the game. Later, when he retired from football, he came up with the idea of the Amateur Cup, a competition for non-professional teams which lasted until 1974, and evening matches played under floodlights, which will probably last forever. Then, during his next career as a referee, Widdowson helped approve the switch from using a white flag to a whistle, and he was even in charge of the first-ever game with proper goal nets. Unbelievable, right?

But by far my favourite of his amazing achievements was this: he invented the shinpad! Yes, in 1874, Widdowson was at the peak of his sporting powers, both in football and cricket, but there was one thing worrying him: injuries. What if he hurt himself and had to stop playing the games he loved? Cricket wasn't too bad because the batsmen wore pads but, in those days, football was pretty brutal. Fouls didn't really exist back then, so players kicked anything they could reach, whether it was the football or a leg ...

A-ha – Widdowson had *another* idea! One day, he took out a pair of his cricket pads and cut them down so that they just covered his shins. Why hadn't he thought of it earlier? It was the perfect protection against dangerous defenders!

At first, the other players couldn't believe it when they saw what Widdowson had strapped to his legs, but they weren't laughing for long. Within a few years, his shinpads were being sold all over England, and footballers have been wearing them ever since. So, the next time you take a nasty kick to the shin, make sure you say a quick thank you to Mr Widdowson because, without him, football would be a lot more painful!

HOW YOU TOO CAN CHANGE THE WORLD

BE KIND AND CARING, BOTH ON AND OFF THE PITCH

Let Rashford inspire you to be the right kind of hero: a football genius *and* a generous person. If someone you know needs help, do what you can to make things better.

DON'T BE SCARED TO SPEAK UP

If you see or hear discrimination, aimed at you or someone else, don't be afraid or uncomfortable to talk about it. It's never right, so report it to the referee, a teacher, or to family and friends.

ALWAYS BE AN ALLY

By showing respect, support and understanding to everyone, whatever their race, gender or religion, you can play your part in the fight for equality. Learn from others about their life stories and experiences, and think about how they compare with your own. Are there any changes you could make to the way you treat people? Embrace the fact that everyone is different, but remember that we should all be united as human beings (and as football fans, of course!).

DON'T GIVE UP ON YOUR DREAM

Always follow your passion, even if it's something that has never been done before and you find obstacles in your way. What you do could inspire other people to follow the same path, just like Rose Reilly and today's Scotland women's team.

AND IF YOU REALLY WANT TO FIGHT FOR WHAT IS RIGHT, WHY NOT START YOUR OWN FOOTBALL TEAM?

As the story of Gandhi shows, sport can be a great way to get people together and spread a powerful message.

CHAPTER TWO

AMAZING ACTS OF KINDNESS

Juan Mata, the Nicest Man in Football

Who is the nicest person in the Premier League?

No, it's not a joke ('Referee Kevin FRIEND!' hahaha); it's a serious question. While there are lots of very kind candidates – my vote for next Prime Minister Marcus Rashford, the always-smiling Son Heung-min, loveable little N'Golo Kanté – my winner would be Manchester United midfielder **Juan Mata.**

The Spaniard is so nice that he sends 'Get Well Soon' messages to injured teammates, and often helps the kit man to unload the bags off the bus after away matches. He even remembers to tweet all of his best friends on their birthdays, sharing funny photos of them when they were young. Awwww, how sweet! Just in case you're still not convinced by Mata's kindness, here's one more example. In 2012, his boyhood club, Real Oviedo, were struggling to stay in the Spanish football league and needed to raise €2 million, so what did he do? He bought shares in the club to keep it going.

Mata's life story is full of good deeds, and he's the perfect proof that nice guys **DON'T** always finish last. In fact, they often finish first – during his incredible club career with Valencia, Chelsea and Manchester United, he has won one Spanish Cup, one EFL Cup, two FA Cups, the Europa League twice, and the Champions League once. Oh, and he also won the 2010 World Cup and Euro 2012 with Spain. Basically, Mata has won just about everything in the game, but he's far too modest to go around boasting about his goal against Italy in the Euro 2012 final, for example, or his crucial equaliser in the 2016 FA Cup final against Crystal Palace.

No, Mata isn't your average modern footballer at all. Instead of playing computer games, he prefers listening to music, experiencing the local culture and learning new things. He writes his own blog (juanmata8.com) and during his time at Valencia and Chelsea, he completed not one but two university degrees (in Marketing and Sports Science).

What a man – clever *and* kind! Instead of only thinking about himself, Mata is all about assisting others and helping those less fortunate than himself.

'My life as a footballer is not normal,' he admitted honestly in an interview on TV in 2016. 'With respect to the world of football, I earn a normal wage. But compared to 99.9 per cent of Spain and the rest of the world, I earn an obscene amount.'

A few weeks later, Mata decided to let his actions speak as loudly as his words. He knew how lucky he was to be living his childhood dream, and he was so grateful for everything that football had given him. Now, it was time to give back.

Mata began his charity work by becoming the first global ambassador for the organisation streetfootballworld. It was the perfect fit. Their mission, like his, was to change the world through football, to 'use football as the universal language to unite the global community to overcome the greatest challenges of our times' – so, for example, using the game's key values of teamwork and fair play to tackle youth unemployment. Mata loved working with streetfootballworld and, soon, he wanted to do more. The organisation had created an amazing team of community projects, which together made a massive difference to so many people's lives. But what if he could do something similar with a squad of fellow superstar footballers? With all their wealth and influence, they could really change the world!

So, in August 2017, Mata decided to launch a new game-changing charity, in partnership with streetfootballworld, called Common Goal.

'THE IDEA WAS "SIMPLE": WHY DON'T WE START SOMETHING THAT HAS NOT BEEN DONE BEFORE IN FOOTBALL, AS A TEAM EFFORT, AND COLLABORATE, PLEDGING 1 PER CENT OF OUR SALARIES TO HIGH-IMPACT ORGANISATIONS THAT USE FOOTBALL AS A TOOL FOR SOCIAL DEVELOPMENT?'

Or to make it even simpler: football for good! The money that Mata's charity raised would be used to fund projects all around the world that used the power of sport to help tackle important social issues such as racism, HIV/AIDS, poverty, gender inequality and youth unemployment. For example, a football club promoting peace in Colombia, South America, by offering young kids an alternative to joining gangs; and a programme in Nigeria, Africa, for girls aged 13 to 19, combining fun football sessions with health education.

It was a brilliant idea, but was it going to work? After setting up the charity, Mata and his co-founder, Jürgen Griesbeck, started asking footballers from all over the world to sign up and join the team. They were asked to donate 1 per cent of their seriously huge salaries – surely that wasn't too much to ask for? German defender Mats Hummels said yes straight away, and so did US soccer stars Alex Morgan and Megan Rapinoe. As word spread, the international dream team grew, player by player:

Goalkeepers: Kasper Schmeichel (Denmark), Alex Rúnarsson (Iceland) and Siobhan Chamberlain (England).

Defenders: Giorgio Chiellini (Italy), Alfie Mawson (England), Kadeisha Buchanan (Canada) and Magdalena Eriksson (Sweden).

Midfielders: Shinji Kagawa (Japan), Dani Olmo (Spain), Caroline Weir (Scotland) and Verónica Boquete (Spain).

Forwards: Serge Gnabry, Timo Werner (both Germany), Paulo Dybala (Argentina) and Pernille Harder (Denmark).

What a squad of superstars, all working together

towards a ... COMMON GOAL! Before long, the team even had a few top managers to choose from – Julian Nagelsmann, Jürgen Klopp or Casey Stoney? That's a really tough choice, or perhaps they could all just work together...

Common Goal now has over 200 members, including players, coaches, YouTube and TV presenters, football executives and organisations. And together, they have donated millions of pounds to organisations in over 200 communities across 90 different countries. In 2020, the charity created a special COVID-19 Response Fund, which has raised over £500,000 to support vulnerable people around the world.

And through his work with Common Goal, Mata has added another trophy to his already-glittering cabinet. In 2019, he received Spain's Queen Sofía award for services to charity. So, let his story be a lesson to us all – you can be a great footballer *and* a great person.

The French Superstar Who Gave Away His World Cup Winnings

Yes, we should all be more like Mata, but when you're the next big thing in football and suddenly you have lots of money and fame, it must be easy to forget about others less fortunate than you. Luckily, that's not the case with France's young superstar **Kylian Mbappé**.

At the 2018 World Cup in Russia, Mbappé stole the show with his magical displays. In the round of 16, he tore Lionel Messi's Argentina apart with his speed and skill, and became only the second teenager ever to score two goals in a World Cup match. The first wonderkid to do it? The King of Football himself, Pelé, way back in 1958!

But Mbappé didn't stop there. He helped lead his country all the way to the final, where they faced Croatia. Wow, France were now just one win away from being crowned World Champions! In the 65th minute, Kylian collected a pass from his teammate Lucas Hernandez in the centre of the pitch, just outside the penalty area. He had Olivier Giroud ahead of him and making a run to his right, but Mbappé only had two things on his mind: 1) shoot, and 2) score. *BANG!* With a whip of his right leg, he fired a swerving long-range rocket into the bottom corner, leaving the Croatia keeper with no chance. *GOAL!* Not only was Mbappé about to win the World Cup at the age of 19, but he had also equalled another of Pelé's achievements. Just imagine being the second teenager ever to score in a World Cup final – that kind of stat could definitely make you a bit big-headed, couldn't it?

Mbappé, however, kept his feet firmly on the ground, and gave all his World Cup winnings away to charity (except for his medal and Best Young Player award, of course!). France's football heroes received a match fee for playing in each of their seven games, plus a big bonus for lifting the trophy. For a star like Mbappé, the total came to nearly £400,000, but winning the World Cup was about the glory, not the riches.

'I EARN ENOUGH MONEY – A LOT OF MONEY. SO I THINK IT IS IMPORTANT TO HELP THOSE WHO ARE IN NEED. A LOT OF PEOPLE ARE SUFFERING, A LOT OF PEOPLE HAVE DISEASES ... IT DOESN'T CHANGE MY LIFE, BUT IT CHANGES THEIRS. AND IF IT CAN CHANGE THEIRS, IT IS A GREAT PLEASURE.'

The charity he chose was Premiers de Cordée, an organisation that offers free sports lessons to children with serious illnesses and disabilities. They run fun sessions in schools, hospitals and, once a year, even in the Stade de France, home of the national football team!

Back in 2017, when he first became a star at Monaco, Mbappé had started looking for a small charity that worked with children in Île-de-France, the region where he was from. Now that the boy from Bondy had grown up to become a superstar, he wanted to give something back to the local community that had created him.

Premiers de Cordée ticked all the right boxes, and

so Mbappé became a patron of the charity. He started making regular visits to meet the kids, sign autographs and even play a bit of football too. 'The objective is to make children smile, that's why I come,' he said. 'So that they forget their everyday problems, and enjoy playing football ... Being handicapped is something difficult. Showing them that they can do sports like everyone is something close to my heart.'

As a high-profile patron, Mbappé has really helped to raise awareness about disability sport, and with his massive donation, Premiers de Cordée have been able to hire more sports coaches and run lots more sessions. It's amazing what one act of kindness from one very famous footballer can achieve.

And Mbappé isn't the only World Cup winner who has made a big donation to charity. Before the start of the tournament in 2014, Germany star **Mesut Özil** teamed up with the sports charity Big Shoe to pay for the surgery of 11 sick children in Brazil, where the World Cup was taking place. 'Why 11?' you might be wondering. Well, that's the number of players in a football team, isn't it?

But when Germany went all the way to the final and won it, Özil used his bonus to pay for the surgery of even more sick children. 'Since the victory of the World Cup is not only due to 11 players but to our whole team, I will now raise the number to 23. This is my personal thank-you for the hospitality of the people of Brazil.'

Mbappé and Özil – two generous football heroes who used their World Cup winnings to give hope and happiness to those who needed it most.

Football, Food and Friendship at the 1991 FIFA Women's World Cup

While we're on the subject of sharing World Cup glory with others, here's a story of incredible kindness from the first-ever official women's competition. After years of tireless protesting and trial tournaments, FIFA finally agreed to host the first Women's World Cup in 1991, over 60 years after the first men's competition. Unbelievably unfair, right? And FIFA didn't even want to call it 'The World Cup'. Instead, the full name was 'The First FIFA World Championship for Women's Football for the M&Ms Cup'. Catchy, eh?

Anyway, the tournament took place in China, with 12 teams involved:

From Asia: China, Japan and Chinese Taipei

From Oceania: New Zealand

From Africa: Nigeria

From Europe: Denmark, Germany, Italy, Norway and Sweden

From South America: Brazil

From North America: USA

It was a massive moment for women's football, and the pressure was on to prove to FIFA that this World Cup (or whatever they wanted to call it!) should be more than just a one-off event. Norway and Sweden were the favourites to win it, but Team USA had lots of talented players, plus two other key things in their favour: fitness and food.

The USA team had played at the 1988 FIFA Women's Invitation Tournament (FIFA really need to work on their names, don't they?), which was also held in China, and they had learned a lot from the experience, both on and off the pitch. On the pitch, they needed to play to their strengths: power and energy. And off it, they needed to bring their own food.

With only a small budget for buying food, the USA team had found eating difficult in 1988. When one of the players found worms in their broccoli – urgh! – they gave up on the local food and lived on fizzy drinks and chocolate instead. As you hopefully all know, that's not a healthy, balanced diet, so three years later, they decided to take their own cooks with them. But no, they hadn't suddenly become highly paid superstars; these cooks were actually just family members who had agreed to do it for free. With suitcases filled with packets of pasta, they travelled together with the team to cheer and feed them all the way to victory.

While the USA players were well-prepared for the World Cup, their opponents weren't. The Sweden team were staying in the same hotel, and when they found out about the secret pasta stash, they cheekily asked if they could have some too. That's a really tough one – what would you say if one of your football club's biggest rivals begged to share your food supplies: 'Sure!' or 'Sorry!'? The USA were even playing against Sweden in their very first group game ...

But remember, this section of stories is about

amazing acts of kindness, and really, all of the teams at the tournament were working together towards the same goal: growing women's football and taking it to the next level. As the USA coach Anson Dorrance says, 'We were part of a culture trying to promote the game internationally, so we fed them.'

And they say footballers are greedy! Well, good things happen to good people. Despite the shared pasta dinner, USA still beat Sweden 3–2, and that was them just getting started. After that, they steamrolled their way past every opponent:

5–0 vs Brazil

3–0 vs Japan

7–0 vs Chinese Taipei

5–2 vs Germany

Full of pasta but still hungry for glory – it turned out to be a real recipe for success. With 22 goals scored in only 5 games, the USA were entertaining everyone (even the old-fashioned men at FIFA) and they were through to the first-ever Women's World Cup final!

There, in front of 63,000 fans, they faced Norway, the team who had won the trial tournament in 1988 (as far as I know, they didn't share their dinner this time). With 15 minutes to go, the score was still 1–1. There could only be one World Cup winner, but which team would it be?

When Shannon Higgins launched a long ball forward, USA attacker Michelle Akers chased after it, using the last of her extra pasta energy. The Norway defender tried to pass the ball back to the goalkeeper, but Akers pounced and beat her to the ball, before tapping into an empty net – 2–1! Soon, it was all over, and the USA were the new World Champions!

After all their wild celebrations on the pitch, the players eventually returned to their hotel to rest. And as the lift door opened, they found a very special banner waiting for them on the floor – the word 'CONGRATULATIONS' spelled out in socks. Wow, who had left such a kind message for them? There was a big clue in the colour of the socks – the yellow of ... Sweden! Yes, despite suffering a frustrating defeat in the semi-finals, they wanted to say well done to the winners (plus thank you for the dinners!). I bet you won't find a better example of sporting behaviour than that.

Entertaining football? Tick! Food and friendship? Tick! The first-ever Women's World Cup had been a huge success, and from there, the competition grew and grew – to 16 teams in 1999, then to 24 in 2015. The audience has grown too; over 260 million people around the world watched the USA beat the Netherlands in the 2019 Women's World Cup final.

Earlier on in the group stage, the USA and Sweden had met for a rematch, 28 years after that first friendly World Cup encounter. This time, the players shared post-match hugs and handshakes, rather than a pre-game pasta dinner, but the final result was the same – another win for the unstoppable USA.

Hurray for the Lockdown Heroes!

During the COVID-19 crisis, lots of us asked ourselves the same question: 'What can we do to help?' Well, as the next three inspiring stories show, the answer is 'lots of different things!', depending on who you are, where you live, and what skills you have to offer.

Let's start with **Gary Mabbutt**, 59, who is a former captain and centre-back for Tottenham Hotspur. You might not have heard of him before, but trust me, he's one of football's good guys. On the football pitch, he was only ever booked 14 times in over 600 games and he was never sent off, which is not bad at all for a defender!

To help you understand a little more about the kind of character he is, here are some other amazing facts about him:

1) At the age of 17, Mabbutt was diagnosed with a disease called type 1 diabetes, and the doctors told him that he would probably have to stop playing professional football. He didn't let that stop him from achieving his dream, though. Mabbutt's motto has always been: 'Do not live your life round diabetes; let it live round you.' So, he took four injections of insulin a day, and on he played for 20 successful seasons, winning the FA Cup with Tottenham in 1991, as well as 16 caps for England.

2) Since he stopped playing in 1998, Mabbutt has bounced back from three major operations. He almost lost a leg in 2011, needed heart surgery in 2017 and then, strangest of all, had part of his foot eaten by a rat in 2018 while on holiday in South Africa! But on he battled because, as you can see, Mabbutt is a very determined man.

When the COVID-19 pandemic began in March 2020, instead of sitting at home bored, he wanted to keep himself busy by doing something useful. But what?

Mabbutt is an ambassador for Tottenham and so he decided to pick up the phone and start calling the club's senior supporters, aged 70 to 99, on their birthdays. It was a chance to say hello and happy birthday, but also to see how they were coping and whether they needed any further help.

Most, however, were in high spirits, especially once they heard it was Mabbutt on the phone! As many of them lived alone, they loved having a long chat with one of their football heroes. Although some fans didn't believe it was really him at first, others kept him on the phone for ages, reminiscing about the good old glory days!

Mabbutt talked and talked, for two or three hours each and every day, using football to help fight loneliness. By June 2020, he had made 250 calls, and by October, he was up to a thousand! What an amazing example of COVID-19 kindness. Mabbutt is hoping that the pandemic 'gives us all a real appreciation of what life is like for others and that we can all pull together as one, to make positive changes wherever they are needed'.

Right, ready for lockdown hero number two? Meet **Lou Macari**, 71, who lives in Stoke and is a former footballer for Celtic, Manchester United and Scotland, as well as a successful manager for Swindon Town and Stoke City.

In 2016, long after his playing and coaching days were over, Macari read a newspaper story about the rising number of homeless people in Stoke. Was the problem really that bad? Yes – when he went out for a walk, he saw the horrible situation for himself: 'It was cold, it was windy, and I thought, "Surely we can do better than this?"'

Macari was determined to do something about it. Thanks to football, he had everything he could have wished for in life, so now he wanted to help others who were having a hard time and give them a fresh start. As soon as he had found a suitable building, he opened the Macari Centre, offering emergency shelter and short-term housing – as well as food and clothing – to people who needed it.

At first, Macari was planning to let a team run the centre for him, but he soon found himself down there every day, speaking to people and solving problems. Once a manager, always a manager, I suppose!

All was going well at the Macari Centre until March 2020, when suddenly COVID-19 changed everything. With its big, shared dormitories that weren't good for social distancing, the government decided that the centre wasn't safe and so it was forced to close. But where would all the residents go? There were over 40 of them living there at the time and they wanted to stay together.

There was no way Macari was going to let them go back to sleeping on the streets again, but what could he do? Luckily, he came up with a marvellous idea one day, as he drove past a field of wooden pods that were rented out as holiday homes: what if he found a massive warehouse and filled it with individual pods like that, which the people could live in instead? Brilliant, that way they could stay together in one place but also live separately, and so help stop the spread of coronavirus!

The plan worked perfectly, and the new residents were delighted with the results. Rather than the large, untidy dormitories that they used to share at the Macari Centre, each now had their own pod to be proud of, with a bed, a heater and even a front door number. That last one might not sound that important, but actually, it means a lot because they would have their own personal address to use when they searched for jobs.

As word spread about the Macari Centre's new home, more and more companies got in touch to make kind donations: 75 duvets from Scotland, 70 mugs from Stoke, and even 46 TVs from Macari's football friends at the League Managers Association.

'The change it's made is incredible,' he explained. Even the messiest of people became much tidier now that they had a pod of their own to take care of. And thanks to the TVs, the residents also knew much more about what was going on in the outside world.

Top job, Mr Macari!

OK, let's move on to the last – and I think most impressive – of our three lockdown heroes: **Aidana Otorbaeva**, 25, who lives in Bishkek, the capital city of the Kyrgyz Republic (a country in Central Asia that sits between Kazakhstan and China) and plays for the national team.

During the summer of 2020, Otorbaeva couldn't concentrate on football because COVID-19 was sweeping through the Kyrgyz Republic and the effects were devastating. Hundreds were dying every day and the hospitals didn't have enough space for all the sick people.

Otorbaeva couldn't bear to just sit and watch her country in crisis, but how could she help? By volunteering on the front line, and also by using her football fame to encourage others to do the same. She was well-known, especially in Bishkek, as a national team player and for signing for Madrid CFF, a professional club in Spain, in 2018. So, she reached out to people through social media, saying:

> **'I AM NOT A DOCTOR ... BUT I AM READY TO VOLUNTEER. TO HELP MEDICAL STAFF, RUN ERRANDS, OR CARRY FOOD. TO MAKE THEIR JOB EASIER, SOMEHOW. I AM NOT ALONE.'**

Otorbaeva was right about that last part. So many people replied, offering their support, that soon she started her own volunteer group called Soobsha, which means 'together' in Russian. And their work began that very night. For the next few weeks, Otorbaeva and the other volunteers risked their own health to help the doctors save lives. They wore full body suits to protect themselves against the virus and even moved into hostels so that they didn't harm their families at home. Although the situation was very scary in the hospitals, they were proud to be playing their part to help their country.

By August 2020, at last the number of COVID-19

cases started to decrease in the Kyrgyz Republic. The worst of the crisis was over, thanks to the heroic doctors and nurses, working together with kind and courageous citizens like Otorbaeva.

'For such a small country with limited resources, volunteers did a colossal amount of work,' medical expert Bermet Baryktabasova said in an article for the American newspaper the *Seattle Times*. 'They saved thousands of lives.'

Otorbaeva is now focused on playing football again, but like so many people, COVID-19 has changed her life forever. 'You understand that there is nothing more valuable than life and health, not even football.'

Through the incredible kindness of its heroes, however, sport can certainly play a part in making the world a better place.

The Unbelievable Acts of Mario Balotelli

For a lot of people, kindness probably isn't the first thing they think of when they hear the name Mario Balotelli. The Italian forward is more famous for helping Manchester City win the Premier League title in 2012, and for his long list of weird and often not-so wonderful stories, which include:

1) Setting off fireworks ... inside. *(Kids, please don't try this at home. It's very dangerous and very stupid!)*

2) Getting a red card for karate-kicking an opponent. *(And don't do this ...)*

3) Throwing darts at youth team players. *(Or this.)*

4) Trying, and failing, to put on a bib. *(Honestly, watch the video – it's hilarious!)*

5) Walking into a school just to use the toilet.

6) Stealing rolling pins from an Indian restaurant in order to have a fake sword fight outside. *(And don't ever steal things either.)*

7) Painting his car in camouflage colours.

8) Celebrating a goal in the Manchester Derby by revealing a message on his shirt that asked, 'WHY ALWAYS ME?'

Good question! But in among all of Balotelli's bizarre behaviour, there are also some amazing acts of kindness. After winning a lot of money at a Manchester casino one night, he handed £1,000 to a homeless person. And when he met a boy who was having a hard time at school, Balotelli decided to go and speak to the bully himself!

But my number one nice story about Balotelli involves his love of animals. When he first moved to Manchester City in 2010, it was a while before his beloved black Labrador, Lucky – whom he'd rescued from a dog's home in Italy – was allowed to join him in England. So, while he waited and kept in touch via video calls, Balotelli volunteered to walk the dogs at his local rescue centre instead. Oh, and he also visited a nearby safari park, where the staff gave him a special tour in a Jeep (best Balotelli quote ever: 'It's not a good idea, I think, to drive a white Maserati into the lion's enclosure') and even let him get in the water and feed the sea lions!

Eventually, Lucky and Balotelli were reunited in England and, after that, nothing could keep them apart. When City won the FA Cup in 2011, Balotelli even asked if his dog could join the team on the open-top bus parade ... and the club said yes!

Fast forward four years and Balotelli was back in the Premier League playing for Liverpool (with Lucky, plus a new pet micro pig called Super!) when the Manchester Dogs' Home was tragically destroyed by a massive fire. A fundraising campaign was set up and it soon reached £1 million, thanks in part to a mystery £25,000 donation. Could it be from Balotelli? ('WHY ALWAYS ME?' hahaha.)

'We can't yet confirm whether he made a donation,' the rescue centre said, 'but he is known as a big dog lover so it would make sense.'

Sadly, the mystery remains unsolved, but my money (sorry, I can't afford £25,000) is still definitely on Balotelli, a footballer equal parts weird and wonderful/ crazy and kind.

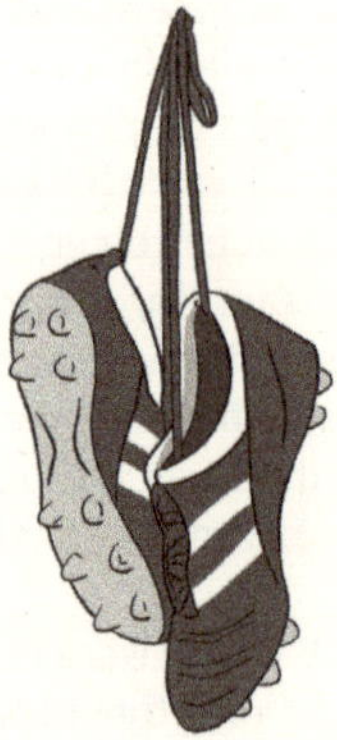

HOW YOU TOO CAN CHANGE THE WORLD

ALWAYS ACT WITH KINDNESS

Whether you're at home, at school or out on the football pitch, it's important to show respect and compassion for your fellow human beings. Remember, everyone is equal.

ONE KIND ACT A DAY IS A FUN GAME TO PLAY!

It could be anything – congratulating an opponent on an awesome goal, helping out your coach by collecting the balls and cones, or thanking the referee at the final whistle. The more random and surprising the better, I say, because then it will definitely put a smile on that person's face.

STAY HUMBLE AND HOPEFUL

Even if you do make it big and become a World Cup winner like Mata, Mbappé and Özil, always remember how lucky you are. Be grateful for your opportunities and look for ways that you could make a difference to the lives of others around the world.

DO WHAT YOU CAN TO HELP

As the stories of Gary Mabbutt and Aidana Otorbaeva show, kindness doesn't have to cost a penny. You can also donate your time and effort to support charities, by helping out with events and spreading the word to all your friends and family.

AND IF YOU DON'T LIKE HUMANS (THAT MUCH), WHY NOT HELP THE ANIMALS INSTEAD?

Balotelli would be delighted, I'm sure ...

CHAPTER THREE

FOOTBALL UNITED (WAR AND PEACE)

Predrag Pašić and the Ladybirds of Peace

One of the best things about football (it's a long list, I know!) is that when you're out there playing on the pitch, nothing else really matters. Any doubts, worries or fears just fade away because you're having fun. And any differences between you and your teammates disappear because you're all working together towards the same aim – winning.

Predrag Pašić is someone who knows all about the power of football to unite people. He was born in 1958 in a big city in Eastern Europe called Sarajevo, which is famous for its beautiful location in the middle of five major mountains, and also for its history (it even has a public toilet that's nearly 500 years old!). Sarajevo is now the capital of a country called Bosnia and Herzegovina, but back then, Bosnia and Herzegovina was one of six republics within a big and very diverse country called the Federal People's Republic of Yugoslavia. People from lots of different ethnic backgrounds and religions lived and played together in harmony – Bosniaks, Serbs and Croats; Christians, Jews and Muslims. Pašić was proud to come from a place so open to everyone, and through his early experiences on the football field, he learned a lot of important life lessons about fairness, justice and friendship: 'We are all part of the same team, and as a team, you win.'

With that attitude, Pašić went on to become a very successful professional footballer, leading his local club FK Sarajevo to the Yugoslav First League title in 1984–85, while also winning the Player of the Season award. He also made ten appearances for the Yugoslavia national team, scoring one goal, and even spent three seasons playing for clubs in Germany.

But by the early 1990s, Sarajevo, Pašić's home, was no longer the same peaceful multicultural place that it used to be. In fact, the whole Federation of Yugoslavia was changing. Each and every country was arguing over whether or not to leave the federation and go it alone.

In Bosnia and Herzegovina, the Bosniaks and Croats wanted to leave the federation, but the Serbs didn't want to separate from Yugoslavia. In 1992, Yugoslav troops attacked Sarajevo to try and stop Bosnia and Herzegovina becoming an independent country. 'The Siege of Sarajevo', as it was called, would end up lasting for almost four years, and over a hundred thousand people died in the civil wars fought in Yugoslavia.

As the conflict continued, several people offered Pašić the chance to leave Sarajevo, but each time, he said no. He wasn't going anywhere; he wanted to stay, and he wanted to help his home city. But with the local people fighting for survival, what could he do to improve their lives and make a positive difference? After thinking long and hard, Pašić decided to focus on what he knew best, what he knew could bring people together – football.

He was going to set up a club, but not for adults: for children. The kids of Sarajevo felt trapped, scared and bored of being inside all day because it wasn't safe for them to kick a ball around on the streets or in playgrounds during the war. As Pašić puts it, 'The children couldn't run, couldn't play, we had to give them power to live.' His new football club would change everything. It would be a place where they could play games without fear of gunfire and feel like normal kids for a few hours.

So, on 15 May 1993, Pašić put out an announcement on a local radio station, inviting children to come with their parents to Skenderija, a complex with an indoor sports hall that had been used during the Winter Olympics in 1984. That would be the home of the new Bubamara Football Club (bubamara means 'ladybird', an insect which brings good luck in Bosnia).

It sounded brilliant, but there was one big problem – Skenderija was in a very difficult and dangerous location. The only way to get there was to race across a bridge and avoid being shot by snipers. Then, once they were inside, there would still be the threat of an attack. Whenever they heard gunfire aimed at the sports hall, the coaches would have to gather up the kids and take them to shelter in a secret tunnel they had found. Sounds scary, doesn't it? Do you think you would risk your life like that to play the game you love?

Pašić hoped that at least 10 or 15 kids would come and join his new football club. On the day of the first training session, however, 200 turned up! He couldn't believe it. They had come from all over the city, and from all different ethnic backgrounds and religions – Bosniaks, Serbs and Croats; Christians, Jews and Muslims. Because at Bubamara, everyone was welcome.

Outside the sports hall, their families might be fighting fiercely against each other but, inside, there was no place for politics or hatred. The children all shared the same pitches, wore the same tracksuits, kicked the same balls, and played on the same teams. Yes, football still had the power to unite them, even while their city was at war.

And football also had the power to help heal their pain and give them hope. For those children, the sports hall became a place filled with dreams, where they were free to run around and lose themselves in the sport they loved. It was a safe space where they could have fun and, for a little while at least, forget the horrible things they had witnessed.

Pašić taught the children of Bubamara the same values that he had learned as a kid through playing the beautiful game: fairness, justice and friendship. And at the same time, he also helped them to develop their football skills. His coaching was a huge success because over 40 of the boys went on to become professional players, with 6 even representing the Bosnia national team! But no matter what level they reached, they would always remember those happy hours they spent at Bubamara Football Club. As one of the Bosnian internationals, defender Veldin Muharemović, says, 'We were so obsessed with sport and football that even if grenades were falling at our feet and bullets were whizzing by, we would have carried on as if nothing was happening. It wasn't until we got home that we realised that the war was going on outside.'

And Pašić's project didn't just stop once the siege ended in 1996. No, instead, it grew and grew, as he helped to form new clubs in other cities across the country, all with the same key message of respect and unity. Bubamara also became the first Sarajevo youth side to play abroad after the war. Their talented team that toured Italy even featured a young striker called Edin Džeko, who would go on to star for Manchester City and Roma, and become Bosnia's most-capped international player, as well as their all-time leading goalscorer.

From all the hardship of the Bosnian War, a golden generation of footballers had emerged. In 2014, Džeko and his countrymen made history when they qualified for the World Cup in Brazil. It was a proud moment for the whole nation, but especially for Pašić. Not only had he played a part himself by coaching Džeko and defender Ervin Zukanović, but the Bosnia team shared the same values as him and his amazing football club.

Just like at Bubamara, everyone was welcome, no matter what their religion or ethnic background. Look what they had achieved. 'This team are a positive example of what we can do when we have no hate between us.'

Pašić watched with delight as that spirit of togetherness spread from the pitch in Brazil to the streets of Sarajevo. During the World Cup, the people of Bosnia came together to cheer on their national team. The power of football had triumphed once again.

> **'EVERYONE KNOWS AND RECOGNISES ME AS A FOOTBALLER, BUT MY GREATEST SUCCESS WAS MY WORK WITH KIDS.'**
>
> – Predrag Pašić

Germany: Divided by Politics, (Re)United by Football

Thomas Müller, Timo Werner, Toni Kroos, Manuel Neuer – these days, we think of Germany as a united and organised match-winning machine. But did you know that between 1949 and 1990, Germany was actually two separate countries with two separate football teams?

Yes, after Adolf Hitler and the Nazis were defeated in the Second World War, the winners, the Allied Forces, decided to divide Germany up between them, like a birthday cake. At first, the country was split up into four zones, each occupied by one of the Allies: the United Kingdom, France, the United States of America and the Soviet Union (now Russia, plus 14 other republics). In 1949, however, the four regions were reduced down to two. The three western parts joined together to form one country, while the eastern part became a separate state, with strong links to the Soviet Union.

The names for these two new countries? Yes, you guessed them, West Germany and East Germany! Despite centuries of shared history, suddenly the two halves were divided by politics. West Germany was a democratic country like the UK, where the people voted for their politicians in elections, and it had a capitalist economy, meaning that businesses had the power to make their own decisions and money. East Germany, on the other hand, was a communist country, where the government owned all the businesses and then shared the money evenly among the people. In 1961, an actual physical barrier was built called the Berlin Wall to separate East and West Berlin, the two parts of Germany's old capital city. The rules were so strict that guards in towers stopped people from crossing from one country to the other, so you couldn't even see your family if they lived on the other side. Can you imagine?

So, that's the history, but what about the football? Well, it was a real tale of two countries. While West Germany went on to win two World Cups and two

European Championships, East Germany only managed to qualify for one major tournament in 40 years. That's partly because their government was more interested in doing well at the Olympics, in events like athletics and swimming, where they could show the world what a strong, healthy country they were. The one football tournament they did qualify for was the 1974 World Cup. And which other country just happened to end up in the same group? Yes, you guessed it again – West Germany!

To make matters even more dramatic, the two Germanys met in the final group game, with first place up for grabs. East Germany won the battle 1–0, but it was West Germany who won the World Cup. Despite finishing second in Group 1, they bounced back to win all their other games, whereas East Germany crashed out in the second round.

Over the years, more and more East Germans tried to escape to the wealthier West, where the grass was greener, the football team was better, and there were more jobs and more freedom. Eventually, due to protests and the collapse of the Soviet Union, in November 1989, the borders were opened, and people began pulling the Berlin Wall down, brick by brick. There was music, dancing and scenes of celebration all along the wall. It was a joyous moment for so many people, as families and friends who had been separated for so long were finally able to meet again. At last, the two Germanys would be reunited!

Well, not quite yet; not on the football pitch, anyway. While the politicians were busy discussing the details of 'New Germany', both national teams were still fighting separately to qualify for the 1990 World Cup. Sadly, it turned out to be the same old story – football success for West and football failure for East.

But all was not lost for the East Germans, or the 'Ossis' as they were known. No, because now that the two regions were reuniting, they could just cheer on West Germany (the 'Wessis') at the World Cup instead. After all, the likes of Lothar Matthäus and Rudi Völler were their brothers, really, rather than their rivals. The team's midfielder Thomas Häßler had even been born within a few miles of the Berlin Wall!

In the past, showing support for West Germany had been strictly forbidden, but now the Ossis no longer had to worry about upsetting the scary secret police who spied on the people of East Germany to make sure that they stuck to the communist rules. Now, they were free to cheer for their fellow countrymen. Yes, thanks to football fever, both sides of Germany were supporting the same team again, after over 40 years apart.

So, 1 July 1990 turned out to be a double celebration day. The two nations agreed that they would join together as one united nation, while on the football pitch, West Germany beat Czechoslovakia 1–0 in the World Cup quarter-finals.

Deutschland! Deutschland!

Three days later, West Germany defeated England in a penalty shootout to reach yet another World Cup final. But this time if the team lifted the trophy, the achievement would mean even more. It would be a win for the whole of the new nation.

A record 28 million Germans tuned in to watch the final on TV, and that figure was only for the West. Thousands more tuned in from the East, as Andreas Brehme scored a late penalty to lead his team to victory against Argentina. It's widely known as one of the worst World Cup finals ever, but why would the Germans care about that? They had won!

Deutschland! Deutschland!

That night, there were fireworks and parties all over 'New Germany', in the East as well as the West. And a few months later, on 3 October 1990, there was more good news to celebrate. It was official – East and West Germany were now one united nation. It was the start of a bright new future for everyone, both on and off the football pitch.

'I'm sorry for the other countries,' Franz Beckenbauer, the Germany manager, announced with confidence, 'but now that we will be able to incorporate all the great players from the East, the German team will be unbeatable for a long time to come.'

Perhaps it was the excitement of winning the World Cup talking, but Beckenbauer had spoken a little too soon. In their first game together as a united national team in June 1991, Germany lost 0–1 to Wales. Then in their first major tournaments, they suffered surprise defeats to Denmark in the Euro 92 final, and then to Bulgaria in the 1994 World Cup quarter-finals.

By Euro 96, however, 'New Germany' had found their top form and, most importantly, their team spirit. While the line-up was still dominated by players from the West, their star player was Matthias Sammer, a sweeper from the East, who had even captained East Germany in their last-ever international match. He was the perfect symbol of the new and united national team that was ready to take Euro 96 by storm. As well as reading the game brilliantly at the back, Sammer also scored two goals in attack as Germany beat England in the semi-finals (on penalties again!) and then the Czech Republic in the final to be crowned Champions of Europe!

The 1990 World Cup had been a massive moment for the new nation, but winning Euro 96 was even bigger because, this time, East and West Germany had done it together, playing side by side. 'The star is the team,' the manager Berti Vogts declared.

> **'FOOTBALL HELPED TO BUILD THE BRIDGE BETWEEN EAST AND WEST GERMANY. AND THE FACT THAT PLAYERS LIKE MATTHIAS SAMMER OR OTHERS CAME TO THE NATIONAL TEAM HELPED A LOT IN THIS CULTURAL CHANGE, BECAUSE THEY WERE IDOLS FOR THE EAST GERMANS.'**
>
> – German captain Jürgen Klinsmann

Yes, as a powerful symbol of national unity, their achievements reached far beyond the pitch. And the Germany team continued to combine players from East and West. In fact, for their opening game against Saudi

Arabia at the 2002 World Cup, they fielded four East Germans in the starting line-up and all four scored in an 8–0 win!

At that tournament, Germany made it all the way to the final, where they lost 2–0 to Ronaldo and Ronaldinho's Brazil (more about them in a few pages). It was a disappointing way to end the World Cup but, together, the team was determined to bounce back better than ever. It took 12 years, but in 2014, Germany thrashed the hosts Brazil 7–1 in the semi-finals, before beating Argentina 1–0 in the final. At last, they were the World Champions again! For their wildly celebrating supporters, it was not only a footballing triumph, but also a huge moment in the country's history. Because Germany had just won their first World Cup as one united nation.

Ronaldo, Ronaldinho, and the Match for Peace

If your nation was in trouble and you needed heroes to save the day, who would you call? The army? The police? Marvel's Avengers? Well, in August 2004, the Caribbean country Haiti decided to bring in a new kind of peacekeeping force: the Brazil national football team.

Haiti is on a beautiful tropical island with turquoise seas, palm trees and rolling green hills. But over the last century, the wealth and natural beauty of Haiti have been badly damaged by many natural disasters, including earthquakes, hurricanes and tropical storms, as well as years of political problems. By 2004, 80 per cent of the population was living in poverty, without access to doctors, schools or a safe place to call home. These people were being denied their basic human rights, and they were determined to fight for them. But the protests got so bad that the Prime Minister, Jean-Bertrand Aristide, fled the country. This led to six months of chaos, with riots and fighting everywhere. The temporary Prime Minister, Gérard Latortue, knew that he had to do something to try to stop the violence, but what? What was so popular that it could help to bring the people of Haiti together? Football!

'A few Brazilian soccer stars could do more ... than thousands of peacekeeping troops,' Latortue said one day, and that got people thinking. When the Prime Minister met with the United Nations and the children's charity UNICEF, together they came up with a clever plan: a 'Match for Peace' between the Haiti national team and Brazil.

'Why Brazil?' you might be wondering. Well, they were the reigning World Champions after beating Germany in the 2002 World Cup final, plus they were also Haiti's favourite football team. Once upon a time, their own national team had been one of the best in the Caribbean. They had played at the 1974 World Cup in Germany, where they even took a surprise 1–0 lead against Italy. Since then, however, football in Haiti had suffered, due to a lack of funding for coaching and clubs for young people. As a result, the national side had failed to qualify for a single major tournament, and so many of the local football fans (glory hunters!) had switched to support another country that they had strong cultural links with, who also happened to be the most successful and entertaining team around – Brazil!

Whenever Brazil played a match, the Haitian people waved their yellow and green scarves with pride, and cheered like crazy. There were pictures of their best players painted on the walls of every Haitian neighbourhood – the legend Pelé, the rising star Ronaldinho and, most popular of all, 'The Phenomenon' Ronaldo.

The Match for Peace was arranged for 18 August 2004 in the capital city, Port-au-Prince. It didn't take long for word to spread far and wide. It was really happening – Ronaldo and Ronaldinho were coming to Haiti! The idea that the world's biggest superstars would be visiting their country was a dream come true for the local people. They couldn't wait to watch Haiti's unmissable match against Brazil. Just imagine the excitement if Kylian Mbappé and the World Cup-winning France national team turned up in your town to play.

Ten giant screens were set up across the country for the special occasion, plus 13,000 locals would get the chance to see the game live inside the national stadium, Stade Sylvio Cator. But who would those lucky supporters be? Not many people in Haiti could afford to pay for tickets, but that didn't matter because the purpose of the match wasn't to make money; it was to promote peace. At first, the plan was that if gang members handed in their dangerous weapons, they would be allowed to enter the stadium for free. Unfortunately, that turned out to be a total disaster because suddenly everyone in Haiti started trying to get guns to exchange for tickets! So instead, the government decided to give the tickets to students from disadvantaged backgrounds and their families.

When the day of the big game arrived, the shops closed

and the fighting paused. Yes, everything else stopped for the most important sporting moment in Haiti's history. For safety reasons, the Brazilian team only flew into Port-au-Prince on the morning of the match, before travelling straight from the airport to the stadium. And instead of a bus waiting to take them there, they found a long line of UN armoured tanks! As they made their way slowly through the city, the streets were lined with thousands of cheering people wearing yellow and green and waving Brazilian flags.

Taking in the views from the top of the tanks, Ronaldo

and his teammates couldn't believe the warm welcome they received – it was like being back home in Brazil, if not even better! They were already putting smiles on people's faces, and the Match for Peace hadn't even kicked off yet. Hopefully with their phenomenal football skills, they could play a part in Haiti's peace process.

It was a scorching hot afternoon in Port-au-Prince as the two teams walked out into the stadium, holding hands with the local kid mascots. Multi-coloured balloons and confetti filled the air – red and blue for Haiti, yellow and green for Brazil, plus white for peace. There was a party atmosphere among the crowd too, where the supporters sent Mexican waves around the stadium and made plenty of noise, especially when Ronaldo showed off the World Cup trophy, which glistened in the summer sun.

Before kick-off, the two teams formed one long line and held up banners in French (the official language of Haiti) and Portuguese (the official language of Brazil), saying:

'SOCIAL JUSTICE IS THE TRUE NAME OF PEACE.'

That day, instead of chaos and conflict, there was happiness and harmony across the country. The people of Haiti came together, united by their love of football.

After hundreds of handshakes, smiles and photos, finally it was time for the game to begin. So, what were Haiti's chances of winning against the World Champions? The answer was somewhere between 'highly unlikely' and 'absolutely impossible'. The only two times they had played against Brazil in the past, they had lost 1–9 and 0–4! Still, football was full of surprises – Haiti had scored first against Italy in 1974, so why not against Brazil 30 years later? And to give his national team even more motivation, Latortue offered a $1,000 reward to any Haitian player who scored in the game.

Sadly, no one was able to collect that prize, but thanks to some heroic defending, Haiti did stop Brazil from scoring for 19-and-a-half minutes. After that, though, the South Americans were just too strong and skilful, especially the two Rs. The crowd cheered wildly for Ronaldo's every trick and flick (and there were lots of them!), but it was Ronaldinho who really stole the show with a superb hat-trick.

His first and third goals were brilliant, but the second was the pick of the bunch, an absolute worldie. When Ronaldo passed him the ball, Ronaldinho dribbled past the first Haiti defender with ease and then did a Maradona/Roulette turn away from two more. *Olé!* Bursting into the box, he beat one more defender and then rounded the goalkeeper, before tapping into the empty net. Unbelievable! And for a little extra entertainment, Ronaldinho celebrated by showing off his samba dance moves.

The match finished Haiti 0 Brazil 6, but the local fans didn't mind at all. In fact, they cheered each and every goal because there were as many Brazil flags waving in the crowd as Haiti ones, if not more!

And besides, the real winner was peace. It was an experience that the people of Haiti had shared together, and one that they would never forget. Once again, football had shown its power to bring unity, as well as joy, to those who needed it most.

Sadly, however, the peace didn't last for long. When the football match ended and the Brazilian stars waved goodbye, it was back to reality for the Haitian people and back to fighting for their basic human rights. The protests continued for years, and then in 2010, the country was hit by its most severe earthquake in over 200 years.

Haiti needed help more than ever, and Brazil was the first country to offer its support. Their government donated $15 million to the cause, and what about their footballers? Well, Ronaldo helped organise a team of heroes to compete in another charity game, this time a 'Match Against Poverty', which took place in Lisbon, Portugal. Brazilians Kaká and Dani Alves both played in the game, which raised over $200,000 to help the people of Haiti.

'I AM VERY KEEN TO GO TO HAITI WITH MY TEAM TO PLAY FOR PEACE.'

– Ronaldo

Pelé's Mysterious African Tour

Ronaldo and Ronaldinho weren't the first Brazilian superstars to help bring peace to the world, however. No, that honour goes to the 'King of Football' himself, **Pelé**. Or does it? You'll have to read on and decide for yourself ...

The year was 1969, and Pelé was a two-time World Cup winner and the most famous footballer on the planet. Everywhere he went, crowds of fans gathered to greet him and watch him play. And in those days, Pelé went to lots of different places, because once his Brazilian club, Santos, had conquered South America, they decided to take on the rest of the world. With Pelé as their star attraction, they knew that they could make lots of money – and friends – by playing football matches in other countries.

On their many tours, Pelé and his Santos teammates

travelled to Europe, North America, Asia, Australia, and then in January 1969, to Africa.

> **'THE OFFICIAL SEASON ACTUALLY STARTS WITH THE FAMOUS [AND STILL MYSTERIOUS] TOUR OF AFRICA. A TOUR SO FULL OF STORIES THAT THERE IS NO CLEAR BOUNDARY BETWEEN LEGEND AND FACT.'**
>
> – Professor Guilherme Nascimento, Author of *Almanaque do Santos FC*

At the time, there were violent conflicts going on in many countries across the continent, including Gabon (homeland of Arsenal's Pierre-Emerick Aubameyang), the Democratic Republic of the Congo (homeland of West Ham's Arthur Masuaku) and Nigeria (homeland of Leicester City duo Wilfred Ndidi and Kelechi Iheanacho).

Many politicians had already tried and failed to end the fighting, but perhaps the world's most famous footballer could do a better job of bringing people together. That was the hope as the Santos team arrived for their grand African tour. After three wins and a draw against teams in the Congo region, they moved on to their second stop: Nigeria.

The country had gained independence from the British Empire in October 1960, but just seven years after that joyous day, a terrible civil war broke out between the different ethnic groups. When the Igbo people tried to create their own separate state called Biafra in the south, the Nigerian government, which was dominated by Nigerian nationalists from the north, fought back. By 1969, millions of people had died from battle injuries and starvation, and yet the civil war continued.

So, was it really a good idea for Santos to visit the country's biggest city, Lagos, during such a turbulent time? What if they made things worse or got caught up in the conflict? After a lot of discussion, it was decided that their match would still go ahead against the Nigeria national team. Hopefully, football – plus Pelé, football's most famous player – could be a powerful tool in bringing peace back to the country.

And did it work? Well, it depends on whose version of the story you believe. According to the Nigerian newspapers, nothing really changed, but according to Santos, when word spread about the arrival of Pelé and co., the warring groups agreed to stop their fighting for two whole days, just so that everyone could enjoy the football in peace. How heart-warming!

The problem is that Pelé himself remembers it slightly differently: 'It is said that there really was a 48-hour ceasefire in the war, made just for us, and my team-mates remember seeing white flags and posters saying there would be peace just to see Pelé play. Well, I'm not sure that is completely true, but the Nigerians certainly made sure the Biafrans wouldn't invade Lagos when we were there.'

What we do know for certain about that game is that it finished in a 2–2 draw and that it was enjoyed by every single one of the spectators at the Lagos City Stadium, who rose to their feet to cheer for all four goals. Oh, and guess who scored both for Brazil? Pelé, of course! Yes, although he was now 29 years old, he was still at the peak of his football powers. In fact, just one year later, he would lead Brazil to a third World Cup trophy in Mexico.

Anyway, back to the myth of Pelé's Match for Peace, or should we say, 'The Mystery of Pelé's Two Matches for Peace'. Yes, you see, after a quick trip to Mozambique, Santos actually returned a week later to play a second match in Nigeria, this time in Benin City. And according to a Brazilian journalist who was there, when Pelé and his teammates arrived in Benin City, the local governor Lieutenant Colonel Samuel Ogbemudia declared a public holiday and even opened the Sapele Bridge to allow Biafrans to come across and watch the match. Then, at the Ogbe stadium, military officers from both sides of the civil war stood together on the touchline in a show of solidarity, and so did the supporters in the stands.

It's a lovely story, and as you've already seen in this book, the beautiful game can definitely be a very powerful tool for peace. But I'm afraid you'll have to make your own mind up once again – true or false, football fact or football myth? Who are you going to believe, a Brazilian journalist who may or may not have been working for Santos, or the greatest player who ever lived? Because while Pelé talks about his trip to Lagos in his autobiography, he doesn't even mention the second match in Benin City . . . With my detective hat on and magnifying glass in hand, I believe this could be for any of the following reasons:

a) Santos won 2–1, but shock horror, Pelé didn't score! So as a striker, it was a game to forget.

b) Memories probably do get a little muddled up when you've played in nearly 1,500 football matches!

c) That's not what happened.

Sadly, we'll never quite know whether Pelé's visit really did unite the people of Nigeria or not, but it certainly inspired the country's next generation of footballers. After the civil war ended in 1970, 'The Super Eagles' (that's the Nigerian national team's nickname) grew stronger and stronger, until at last in 1994, they finally qualified for their first-ever World Cup. And at the tournament in the USA, Nigeria even went on to top their group ahead of Diego Maradona's Argentina. Although they lost to Italy in extra-time in the round of 16, the Super Eagles had impressed everyone, including Pelé.

Back in 1974, he had predicted that an African nation would win the World Cup by 2000, and now Nigeria were looking the most likely team to do it. Unfortunately, the Super Eagles have still never got past the second round, but it's good to know they have Pelé's special support. In 2002, when the legend was asked to select the 50 best players in the world, he made sure to include one Nigerian on his list: Jay-Jay Okocha. And who had been Okocha's childhood football hero? Pelé, of course!

The Lions Who Refused to Lose

Football heroes come in all kinds of shirts and sizes, and from all over the world, but if you ask me, nothing beats a bunch of proud international players who bring hope and joy to their country during troubled times. So, it's my great pleasure to introduce you to the inspirational Iraq national football team of 2007.

That year, the 'Lions of Mesopotamia' were preparing to play in the latest edition of the Asian Cup, their region's biggest football tournament. However, it was very hard for the players to focus on football when their country was at war, both with other nations and with itself. Iraq is a country in Western Asia, which is part of the Middle East region, along with its neighbours Iran, Turkey, Jordan, Syria and Saudi Arabia. In 2003, a US-led force had invaded Iraq with the aim of overthrowing their controversial president, Saddam Hussein. Although they succeeded, the consequences were devastating for the country. Thousands of Iraqis died in the conflict, which lasted for years and led to a civil war between the nation's main ethnic groups: the Sunni and Shia Muslims, and the Kurds.

Violence, danger and destruction had become an everyday experience for the people of Iraq, and their beautiful country, with its amazing mountain ranges, rivers and large desert landscapes, was in ruins. By the beginning of 2007, their football team was in tatters too. After losing to Saudi Arabia at the Arabian Gulf Cup in January, coach Akram Salman had been sacked, and five months later, there was still no one new to replace him. Every manager they asked said no until eventually, with just weeks to go until the start of the Asian Cup in Indonesia, Brazilian Jorvan Vieira finally agreed to take the job.

At least now they had someone in charge, but leading Iraq to victory really did look like mission impossible for Vieira. Yes, the Lions had been a pretty talented team at the time of the US-led invasion – they had made it to the quarter-finals at the last three Asian Cups in a row – but since then, the conflict had changed everything. The Iraqi Premier Football League had been destroyed, FIFA had banned them from playing international matches at home in Baghdad because it wasn't safe, and whenever the team trained, the sound of gunfire and missiles was always in the air. For the players, most of whom had lost friends or family members in the fighting, it was a constant reminder of the war.

Still, despite all their troubles on and off the football pitch, the Iraq national team had a major tournament to prepare for. While the players were excited about the upcoming Asian Cup, they weren't expecting to stay in Indonesia for very long. They would be up against much stronger and more stable teams such as Japan, South Korea and Australia, as well as their local rivals Saudi Arabia and Iran. And when they barely had enough kits for everyone to wear, how were Iraq expected to compete?

What they did have plenty of, though, was team spirit. Vieira had noticed it straight away, and he knew what a powerful weapon it could be, more effective than any clever tactic or substitution. Tragedy and hardship had brought the Iraqi players together, building an unbreakable bond between them. With Sunni captain Younis Mahmoud playing alongside Kurdish midfielder Hawar Mulla Mohammed and Shia goalkeeper Noor Sabri Abbas, they represented a beacon of hope and unity during their country's darkest times. No matter what their religious, ethnic or cultural differences, they were one united football team. And now, through their performances on the pitch, they had the chance to bring happiness to all the people who were suffering back home.

A 1–1 draw with Thailand wasn't the dream start they were hoping for, but never mind, Iraq still had two more group games to go, starting with Australia. Although 'The Socceroos' were one of the favourites to win the whole tournament, that didn't scare the Lions of Mesopotamia.

In the 60th minute, the match was tied at 1–1 again, when Mahmoud won the ball and raced forward on the attack. After a neat bit of hold-up play, he passed to Nashat Akram, who threaded a beautiful ball through to Mulla Mohammed, who calmly poked a shot past the keeper – *2–1!* It was one of Iraq's greatest-ever goals and, to make it even better, Mulla Mohammed celebrated with one of the best somersault-forward roll combos you're ever likely to see. Seriously, check out the video ...

So, could the Lions hold on to secure a famous and surprising victory? Oh, they could do better than that! In the 85th minute, super sub Karrar Jassim tapped in to make it 3–1. Game over – against the odds, Iraq had their first win at the tournament. And following a 0–0 draw with Oman, they even finished top of Group A.

So far so good, but next up for Vieira's band of football brothers was a quarter-final against Vietnam. Could they finally break their 35-year curse and reach the Asian Cup semi-finals? Yes! Mahmoud was their

man of the match this time, scoring both goals in a comfortable 2–0 win. The second was a fantastic free-kick and, as the ball hit the back of the net, 'The Desert Fox' (one of football's best nicknames, don't you think?) took off his captain's armband and held it to his forehead like a bandana, showing off the Iraqi national flag in the centre. It was a joyous moment for the hundreds of supporters in the stadium, and for the millions more at home.

At last, the Lions had made it through to the semi-finals, but they weren't stopping there. Although they hadn't entered the tournament with much hope, their confidence had grown with every game and every win. So yes, of course they could beat South Korea – they believed they could beat anyone as long as they worked together as one united team. And as long as they had their beloved, broken country cheering them on.

In the end, the semi-final went all the way to a penalty shootout but, despite the extra pressure, the Iraqi players held their nerve. They hadn't forgotten their mission to make their nation happy. Once again, it was one big team effort. All four takers scored their spot-kicks, and then goalkeeper Abbas made a super save to stop Yeom Ki-hun. Those brave and determined Lions had done it; they were through to the Asian Cup final!

There were scenes of celebration at the Bukit Jalil National Stadium in Kuala Lumpur, and back home on the streets of Iraq too. The people hugged, sang and waved their national flags together with pride, and it was all thanks to their fantastic football team. They were now one win away from lifting the Asian Cup – what an achievement it would be!

Sadly, however, the joy didn't last long. That night in Baghdad, 50 cheering fans were killed by bombs and gunfire. When the Iraqi players heard the terrible news, they thought about pulling out of the Asian Cup final. After all, they didn't want to be the cause of more people dying. But when the mother of one of the victims begged them to continue in his memory, the team agreed to play on.

'WE KNEW WE HAD TO WIN THE MATCH FOR HER AND SO MANY OTHER PEOPLE.'

– Younis Mahmoud

After all, their success was about something much more important than just football; it was about national unity. With every victory on the pitch, they were sending out a powerful message about what was possible when everyone put aside their differences and worked together. As Mahmoud would later say, 'It doesn't matter what I am. Above all else, I am Iraqi.'

So, could the team finish what they'd started and bring the Asian Cup home? Their opponents in the final would be Saudi Arabia, the same side they had lost to six months earlier at the Arabian Gulf Cup. A lot had changed since then, however. The Lions of Mesopotamia were now a totally different team, and more motivated than ever to win. As the game went on, Iraq grew stronger and stronger. They were creating lots of good chances but all that was missing was a winning goal ...

Then, with 20 minutes to go, it finally arrived. Mulla Mohammed curled a high corner towards the back post, and up leaped their leader Mahmoud to head the ball home. What a hero! The Iraq captain ripped off his armband once again and waved it above his head as he raced over to celebrate with the supporters. When at last the final whistle blew, Iraq were the winners, the new Champions of Asia!

It was an astonishing achievement from an extraordinary group of players, who had overcome so many obstacles in order to unite their country and make the people proud. As Mahmoud lifted the trophy high above his head in Jakarta, fireworks exploded in the sky. And back home in Baghdad, Basra and many other Iraqi towns and cities, thousands of people forgot about their differences and partied together in the streets. For once, their country was celebrating a win, rather than mourning its losses, and so they danced, waved flags and honked their car horns. Having been through so much, they were determined to make the most of this moment of sporting glory. Yes, thanks to football, 29 July 2007 was a night that the Iraqi people would never forget.

'I THINK EVERYONE IN THIS WORLD HAS TO DO SOMETHING TO HELP SOLVE THESE PROBLEMS. I DON'T HAVE A GUN, I HAVE A BALL AND WHISTLE. THIS IS MY WAY, TO GET MY PLAYERS MORE TOGETHER TO SHOW THE PEOPLE OF IRAQ THAT WE CAN LIVE TOGETHER WITHOUT ANY PROBLEM.'

– Manager Jorvan Vieira

Family vs Football

Real Madrid vs Barcelona, Liverpool vs Everton, Celtic vs Rangers, Garrison Gunners vs Woolpack Wanderers (they're the only two teams in the Isles of Scilly Football League so they have to play against each other 17 times every season!) – as we all know, football rivalries can be really fierce. But surely you would put those feelings to one side if it meant saving a family member's life? Well, yes and no, in the case of brothers Paul and Martin Warburton from Manchester.

You see, Paul grew up as a proud 'Blue', a City supporter, while Martin decided to be a 'Red' instead, a fan of their local rivals, United. For a long time, this conflict didn't really cause too many issues, other than a bit of family tension on Manchester Derby day.

In 1997, however, Paul was sadly diagnosed with leukaemia and, six years later, he needed a life-saving transplant. When

Martin turned out to have the matching RED stem cells, he was happy to help his older brother, but he had an idea:

'This was the perfect chance to get Paul to stop backing the Blues and switch over to the almighty Reds.'

Before Martin said yes, Paul would have to agree to some hilarious conditions:

1) He had to stop supporting City, and laugh as they got relegated.
2) He had to become a United fan instead, joining the Manchester United FC Supporters' Association and signing up to the club's television channel, MUTV.
3) He had to repaint his house red and wear mostly red clothes, in honour of his new favourite team.
4) He could only use blue-coloured materials 'as rags to clean up dirt'.

Surely Martin was just joking around? Well, maybe, but he still presented his brother with a proper contract! And eventually and reluctantly, Paul agreed to sign it. He didn't have much choice, though, did he? It was a life-or-death situation!

Luckily for him, the terms of the contract didn't turn out to be too painful. For the next three seasons, it was Arsenal and Chelsea who won the league title, not Martin's United. And Paul's secretly still-beloved City have never been relegated since. In fact, in 2008, the club was bought by the very rich

Abu Dhabi United Group, who helped take them from an average mid-table team to 2012 Premier League Champions. And who did they beat to the title on goal difference that year? Yes, United – I bet Martin was SEEING RED (geddit)! His comedy contract had turned out to be a curse.

So, let that be a lesson to you all – always keep football and family separate!

'I have always been of the view that younger brothers are there as spares, but he has proved to be a bit more useful than that.'

– Paul Warburton

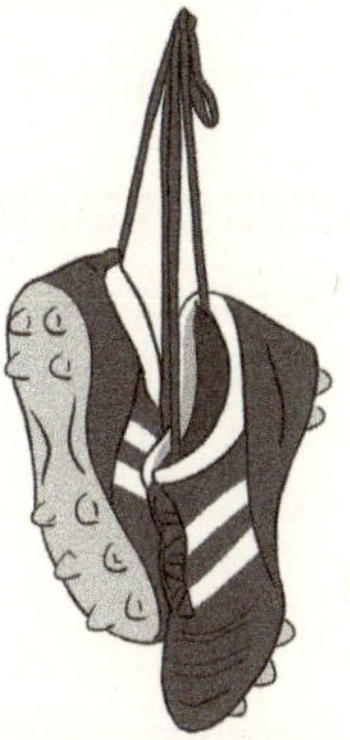

HOW YOU TOO CAN CHANGE THE WORLD

BE A GOOD/KIND TEAMMATE

Teamwork is so important both on and off the football pitch. As you've seen throughout the stories in this section, it's amazing what we can achieve when we work together.

... AND A GOOD/KIND OPPONENT

By showing respect for those you play against – shaking hands and saying, 'Well done!', whether you win or lose – you can help set a great example for others to follow.

MAKE PEACE, NOT WAR!

If something or someone makes you angry on the football pitch, just let it go and get back to having fun. And if you see other people fighting or arguing around you, do your best to calm them down and make things better. Just like Germany, a united team is always a better team.

MAKE SURE EVERYONE'S WELCOME!

If you see a new kid in the school playground, why not go over, say hello, and invite them to join in your football game? Small gestures of kindness/friendship like that can make a massive difference. So, be more Bubamara!

BRING JOY THROUGH FOOTBALL (AND/OR FOOD)

If someone you know is having a hard time, think of ways that you could cheer them up. What do they enjoy most? If they're a football fan, then maybe you could entertain them with your skills like Ronaldinho in Haiti and Pelé in Nigeria. If not, in my experience you can't go wrong with a yummy chocolate cake!

CHAPTER FOUR

PROTECTING THE PLANET

The Greenest Football Team the World Has Ever Seen

Our planet is getting hotter and hotter, and not in a 'Great, let's all go on holiday!' way. No, rising temperatures are leading to more extreme and unpredictable weather, which in turn is leading to floods, droughts and the loss of animal habitats.

And what's causing all this climate change? We are. By burning too many fossil fuels like oil and gas, cutting down too many trees, and farming too many cows (when they burp and fart, they produce a harmful gas called methane), we humans are seriously damaging Planet Earth, which really doesn't seem fair. As the Swedish environmental activist Greta Thunberg said in 2019, 'We deserve a safe future. And we demand a safe future. Is that really too much to ask?'

OK, so what can we do to protect our planet? Well, all of us must play our part, but football has a particularly big responsibility. Every time your favourite team flies to an away match or your favourite player travels by private jet, they're burning lots of fuels and producing lots of carbon dioxide (CO_2). In fact, the world's top 20 footballers alone produce over 500 tonnes of CO_2 emissions every year, which is more than most entire countries.

Football simply can't continue like this. If it does, the rising temperatures will cause serious problems, with players and supporters overheating, while droughts could destroy local grass pitches. Plus, in England, there's a chance that heavy rain and flooding could leave 23 of the 92 league stadiums at least partly underwater by 2050, including Southampton's St Mary's and Chelsea's Stamford Bridge.

So, with their future under threat, football clubs are looking for clever new ways to become greener and more sustainable. For example, Manchester United have made the rubber surface at the edge of their Old Trafford pitch from recycled old trainers, while four

Premier League teams – Arsenal, Liverpool, Tottenham and Southampton – have signed the UN Sports for Climate Action Framework to tackle climate change and become carbon neutral by 2050. These are all positive signs of progress, but there's only one football team who have been fighting to protect the environment for years – **Forest Green Rovers**.

Who? If you don't already know, Rovers are a League Two club from Nailsworth in Gloucestershire, which is officially the smallest town ever to have a team in the English Football League. Cool fact, right? But wait until you hear about all the awesome work these eco-superheroes are doing to save our planet ...

It all started in 2010 when Dale Vince, owner of Ecotricity, the world's first green energy company, became the major shareholder and new chairman of the club. At that time, Rovers were a non-league team in trouble. The only reason they hadn't been relegated from the Football Conference that season was because another club, Salisbury City, had broken the rules and so were sent down instead.

Fortunately, Vince was a (chair)man with a grand plan – to take Rovers up into the Football League, while also turning them into 'the world's greenest football club'. There were three parts to his plan:

1) **FOOD!** For starters, the players were banned from eating red meat, and so were their supporters at the New Lawn stadium. From now on, they would only be serving vegetarian food, or eco-friendly chicken and fish, at Forest Green Rovers. Fancy! Then in 2015, the club took all animal products off the menu, becoming the world's first fully vegan football club. Not only is the food better for the environment, but it's also better for the players because it's a lot quicker to digest ahead of a big game of football. The fans love it too – the 'Q Pie' (made from Quorn, rather than meat) is now one of the most popular matchday meals in England!

2) **ENERGY!** The club started using cow poo to care for their pitch instead of nasty chemicals, set up a clever system to recycle rainwater, and put 180 solar panels

on the stadium roof. Rovers already ran on 100 per cent green energy and 0 per cent fossil fuels, but this way, the club would be able to generate 10 per cent of their electricity from the sun. The result of that extra energy? A solar and wind-powered robot lawn mower, nicknamed 'The MowBot'!

3) **TRAVEL!** Rather than each of them driving to and from training on their own, the Forest Green

players grouped together to share cars and save the environment. In 2013, the club also partnered with the car manufacturer Nissan so that the team could test-drive their new all-electric vehicles. Plus, they added electric car charging points outside the stadium to encourage fans to travel to games in an eco-friendly way too.

The crowning glory came in 2018, when the United Nations officially announced Forest Green as the world's first carbon-neutral football club. That's right, thanks to all their environmental efforts, they were now absorbing as much CO_2 as they were releasing.

It was great that Rovers were top of the green table, but how were the football team performing on the pitch? Well, after another seven frustrating seasons in the Conference, Rovers were finally promoted to the Football League in 2017, for the first time in their 129-year history.

What an achievement! But after enjoying their play-off win at Wembley, Vince got straight back to building the football club of the future. The next steps? A new kit made from 100 per cent coffee waste and recycled plastic (the current shirt is made from 50 per cent bamboo, which they also use for the players' shinpads), an electric team coach, and then hopefully by 2025, a new stadium, called 'Eco Park', which will be made almost entirely out of wood and surrounded by 500 trees. Plus, on the pitch, the team are aiming for promotion all the way up to the Premier League, of course!

The Forest Green way is clearly working well, so will other clubs follow in their zero-carbon footprints? We'll have to wait and see but, as Vince says, there's no time to waste in the fight against climate change. Football must tackle the issue today, not in the future: 'We have ten years and if we don't start now it's just going to get harder.'

Did you hear that, world of football? Hopefully, other clubs are listening and will be inspired to take serious environmental action too. But in the meantime, let's show our support for the team who led the way. A zero-carbon footprint *and* a zebra-pattern home shirt? Yes, I'm a Forest Green Rovers fan from now on!

'I HAD TO BRING ALL OF OUR LEARNINGS IN ENERGY, TRANSPORT AND FOOD, OUR ETHICS AND OUR SUSTAINABLE APPROACH TO ACTUALLY CREATE A GREEN FOOTBALL CLUB.'

– Dale Vince

Héctor Bellerín, the Footballer Who's Not Afraid to Branch Out

While we're on the topic of the mighty Forest Green Rovers, do you know which footballer recently became the club's second biggest shareholder? The answer is …

Arsenal and Spain star **Héctor Bellerín**! Since his move from Barcelona back in 2013, the speedy right-back has become a fans' favourite for the Gunners, winning three FA Cups, as well as four caps for his country. On the field, he's a red, but off it, he's been going green for years.

That's why Héctor and Forest Green Rovers really is a football match made in heaven. He first decided to stop eating meat and become a vegan back in 2016. When he told his mum, she was really worried. 'But Héctor, you hate vegetables!' she said. He stuck to his vegan diet, though, because he noticed a big difference straight away. He felt fitter, stronger, and he was no longer getting as many injuries. But for him, it wasn't just about better performances on the football pitch; it was also about protecting the planet for future generations.

Bellerín's passion for the environment began as a kid growing up in Barcelona, a city by the sea. He loved nature and, in the springtime, he spent many happy hours helping his grandfather plant trees in his garden. Then, when summer came around, Héctor would head to the local beaches, but every year, he noticed that the natural beauty was being ruined by more and more rubbish. People left their food wrappers and plastic bottles everywhere – all across the sand and even in the water. Not only was it an ugly sight to see, but it was also dangerous for the sea creatures, who could swallow or choke on them.

That wasn't the kind of world that Bellerín wanted to pass onto future generations, and so he began to make changes to his lifestyle. He became a vegan, stopped using so much plastic, and bought himself an electric car. These were all positive steps towards saving the planet, but he couldn't tackle climate change on his own. It was an issue that affected the whole world, so what else could he do to help spread the word?

'WITH SOCIAL ISSUES, I THINK AS FOOTBALLERS WE HAVE A MASSIVE PLATFORM THAT WE SHOULD BE USING WAY MORE THAN WE ACTUALLY ARE.'

In 2018, Bellerín began to use his powerful voice to speak out – about women's rights, racism, and especially about the environment. In a really interesting interview with the Arsenal website, he urged people to keep making small changes to their lives – like picking up litter, recycling, turning off taps, saving electricity – because:

'If everyone takes that same action for good, it can save tonnes of water, plastic, animals.'

Yes, some of Bellerín's followers told him that he should stick to football, but most listened to his message. After all, he wasn't talking about totally transforming the way we live; he was talking about making small changes that could have a big collective impact. What he said made sense, and it made football fans think:

'We're killing so many forests because we want more money, but if there's no Earth, there's no money to spend.'

As well as raising awareness about environmental issues, Bellerín also decided to take further action. When Premier League football returned in June 2020, he teamed up with a charity called One Tree Planted to make an exciting new promise:

'For every Arsenal game we win this season I will plant 3,000 trees to help combat the carbon emissions issues we have.'

Wow, if the Gunners won all of their remaining ten league matches, then that would mean ... 30,000 trees planted! That was never going to happen (sorry, Arsenal fans!), but they did beat:

1) Southampton

Héctor posted a GIF of a plant being placed in the soil.

2) Norwich

3) Wolves

'More trees more life!' he tweeted.

4) Leicester

Actually, Arsenal only drew this game, but afterwards, Bellerín decided, 'Personally feel we didn't deserve that result last night. Tough to take after the fight and courage from the whole team, therefore I will still plant those trees!'

5) Liverpool

6) Watford

So, 6 league wins + 3 more victories as Arsenal won the FA Cup = 9. And 9 x 3,000 equals? 27,000! But in fact, thanks to lots of kind donations from other people, Bellerín was able to announce in August:

'50,000 TREES PLANTED' – what an amazing addition to the Amazon Rainforest in South America!

And just two months later, Héctor made his next

contribution to the fight against climate change by joining the Forest Green Rovers family. 'It's important that I invest in things I am passionate about,' he said, 'and I'm excited to help push football into having a sustainable future.'

You might think that was more than enough environmental work for one famous footballer, but no, Bellerín likes to keep himself very busy. In 2021, he announced another new project, this time involving his other great passion – fashion. He gets his love of cool clothes from his mum, Maty, who makes her own designs from scratch, sometimes with the help of her son. However, this time, Héctor was teaming up with the massive brand H&M to design a new collection of clothes which all had one thing in common: they were made from recycled and organic materials. So, all natural, with no need for chemicals!

While Bellerín is probably the most famous 'green' footballer, he's far from the only one. For example, his former Arsenal teammate **Mathieu Flamini** now runs a really successful company that makes environmentally friendly materials to use instead of plastic. Roma defender **Chris Smalling** has become a vegan like Bellerín, and he's also invested in a company that uses pineapples to make a sustainable substitute for leather!

And finally, Leeds United striker **Patrick Bamford** started showing off a new goal celebration last season, where he makes a 'Z' shape with his fingers. Want to know what it means? 'This is the bolt. It's a symbol for the planet, a force of nature and the symbol of Hylo Athletics' [a sportswear company who sponsor Bamford] mission using sport to inspire positive change for our planet.'

The Denmark Midfielder Determined to Make a Difference

Sunday 24 March 2019 was a momentous day for Juventus Women. For the first time ever, they played a match at the Allianz Stadium, the home of the men's team, in front of 39,000 fans, a new Italian record. Thankfully, the match finished Juventus 1 Fiorentina 0, and who grabbed the winning goal in the 84th minute? No, not English striker Eni Aluko or Italian attacker Barbara Bonansea, but Danish defensive midfielder **Sofie Junge Pedersen**, pouncing at the back post to head the ball home. She doesn't score many, so this one was extra special, and as you're about to find out, it couldn't have happened to a nicer hero.

You see, when she's not scoring winners or working hard to win the ball back out on the pitch, Pedersen is helping others and tackling climate change instead. As a child, she was lucky enough to travel the world with her family, visiting amazing places in Africa, Asia and South America. She enjoyed all of her exciting adventures, but they also made her appreciate how lucky she was to live in a wealthy country like Denmark. So, as soon as she became a very successful professional footballer, Pedersen wanted to do whatever she could to help.

'INEQUALITY TOGETHER WITH CLIMATE CHANGE ARE THE TWO MOST IMPORTANT PROBLEMS TO SOLVE IN THE WORLD, I THINK.'

First, Pedersen decided to focus on fighting inequality and poverty. For years, she has been assisting refugees in Denmark and disadvantaged kids in Ghana, and in 2018, she joined Common Goal, Juan Mata's football charity that we focused on earlier in this book.

At the same time, through making small, simple changes in her daily life, Pedersen also did what she could to protect the planet. For example, she stopped eating red meat, using single-use plastics like bottles, and buying new clothes that were bad for the environment. As a top footballer, she still had to take lots of planes to play in international matches, but she tried her best to travel as little as possible. And every time she did fly, she 'offset' her carbon emissions, which means that she paid to remove the same amount of CO_2 that her journey produced, by, for example, planting new trees like Bellerín. Forests for fumes – what a substitution!

For the moment, however, football is still Sofie's main focus. As well as winning trophies with Juventus, her next aim will be winning the UEFA Women's Euros with the Denmark national team. Those are her sporting goals, but they sit side by side with her social goals, like teammates in the changing room. 'I could be able to achieve my dreams on the football pitch by being a very selfish person, but I don't want to be a selfish person,' she says. 'I have defined some values for myself and one of those three values that I have – and try to act on – is to be a contributing person.' That means lots of tireless running, tough tackling and midfield battling to help her team to win on the football pitch, while also helping others and protecting the environment. What an all-action hero!

So, when Pedersen heard about a new programme called Football4Climate, it sounded like the perfect way to combine her passions. She couldn't wait to sign up, get involved and help spread the word. Not only is Football4Climate raising awareness of environmental issues, but it also offers useful ideas for how football clubs can change and play a part in tackling the climate-change problem, rather than making it worse, such as removing all single-use plastic in stadiums and signing up to the UN Sports for Climate Action Framework.

It's not all about the top teams, though; there's also lots of useful information for us supporters in the Football4Climate Fan Club. You can download a letter to sign and send to your club asking them to take action, plus calculate your personal carbon footprint by answering questions about your home, transport and lifestyle. Give it a go! Remember, as we saw in the story of Forest Green Rovers, how you travel to matches and what you eat in the stadium can have a big impact on the environment.

As an ambassador for Football4Climate, Sofie has spoken at lots of events, and she's committed to doing whatever she can to help protect our future, before it's too late. And she's not the only top female footballer tackling climate change. New Zealand and Lewes FC forward **Katie Rood** has teamed up with Planet Super League, a fun online tournament where fans compete to win points for their favourite club by doing environmentally friendly activities such as walking, running, saving energy at home or going meat-free for a week. You can win trophies and prizes for yourself along the way but, just like with football, it's all about the team who finishes top of the table at the end of the season. Last year, that was Leicester City, but why not help your club to win next time around, while saving the planet at the same time?

Through programmes like Football4Climate and Planet Super League, football is finding exciting new ways to spread the message that saving the environment is one big team effort. It's essential work, but it can be fun too, and hopefully the more top players like Pedersen and Rood speak up and show their support, the more fans all over the world will listen. Come on, we can win this, Football United!

Creating Cool Kits Out of Ocean Waste

So far in this section, we've heard about what football clubs and players are doing to protect the planet. But what about other areas of the sports industry, such as the clothing companies that make football kits? We all look forward to seeing our club's new designs each season, don't we, but have you ever thought about where your favourite shirt actually comes from?

At the moment, most kits are still made from polyester and nylon because they don't trap sweat and heat in the same way as natural materials like cotton. However, these synthetic fabrics are usually produced through a chemical reaction involving oil, which makes them bad for the planet. So, what other materials could we use instead to make more eco-friendly football kits? Well, the company PlayerLayer used a 50 per cent bamboo mix for their 2019 Forest Green Rovers home shirt, while **Adidas** have teamed up with an American environmental organisation called **Parley for the Oceans** to create sportswear out of the over five trillion pieces of plastic that are floating in our seas.

Five trillion?! Yes, you read that number right – sad and really scary, isn't it? That's why eco-friendly footballers like Bellerín and Pedersen are saying 'No!' to single-use plastic. And Parley for the Oceans are trying to fight the problem too, by encouraging big companies to explore new ways to create their products which don't harm the planet. Their partnership with Adidas started on Earth Day (22 April, by

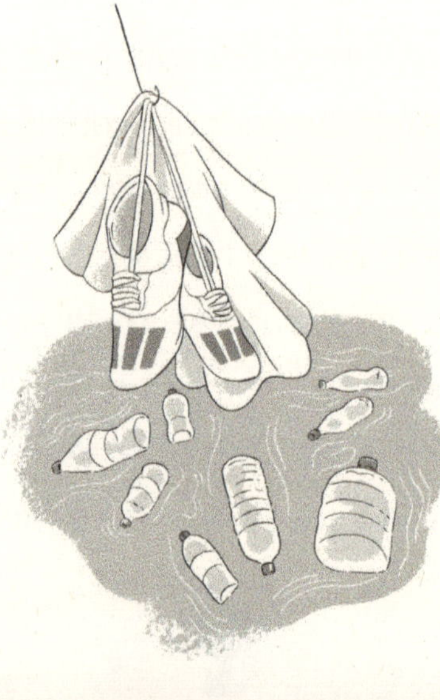

the way) in 2015 and it has two main aims:

1) to prevent plastic from entering our oceans and
2) to turn the plastic that does enter our oceans into sportswear

It's an excellent idea, and here's the simple science of how it works:

Step 1: Parley pay a team of local workers in the Maldives (a chain of small islands just south of Sri Lanka and India) to clean up the coastal areas and collect up all the plastic waste that they find, including bottles, bags, straws, toothbrushes, plus illegal deep-sea fishing nets which kill over 100,000 animals each year.

Step 2: The plastic is then sent to Taiwan, where it is shredded and reworked into polyester yarn.

Step 3: The polyester yarn is then used to make Adidas clothing and trainers.

Step 4: The clothing and trainers are bought by customers, but not in plastic bags.

Cool, right? Within a year, Parley and Adidas had

produced more than 7,000 pairs of the special Ultra Boost trainers, and they now make 15 million pairs of shoes a year.

From sports shoes, they soon moved onto their next impressive product: football kits. In 2016, two of the biggest clubs in the world showed off Parley shirts made from recycled plastic, with the words 'FOR THE OCEANS' printed on the inside of each collar. First, Robert Lewandowski's Bayern Munich wore theirs in a 1–1 draw with Hoffenheim on 5 November. Then, three weeks later, Cristiano Ronaldo's Real Madrid wore theirs in a 2–1 win over Sporting Gijón. And best of all, the clubs' fans could buy and wear them too.

At first, the shirts were only used for one-off matches, but for the 2018–19 season, Adidas launched new Real Madrid and Manchester United third kits made from Parley plastic. The Real shirt was even a coral pink colour, a reference 'to the beauty of the oceans that we need to protect'.

As well as product design, education is another key

part of the Parley for the Oceans project, and working with massive football clubs is a brilliant way to spread their environmental message far and wide. When the Manchester United, Real Madrid and Juventus players visited the USA on pre-season tours in 2018, they were all invited to 'Parley Ocean School' events.

'Really interesting day with Parley and Adidas learning about the risk of plastic pollution,' Juan Mata posted to his millions of Instagram followers around the world to raise awareness of the problem.

And the good work goes on. Through their partnership with Parley, Adidas have promised to make all of their products out of 100 per cent recycled polyester by 2024. So, it shouldn't be long before we're all buying their first eco-friendly football boots!

'IF WE WERE ABLE TO GET OUR MESSAGE ACROSS USING THE BEAUTIFUL GAME, WE WILL REALLY BE ABLE TO MOVE THE NEEDLE.'

– Cyrill Gutsch, Parley founder

The Former England Captain Creating a Buzz

Did you take up any new hobbies while you were stuck at home during the COVID-19 lockdown?

Drawing, perhaps?

Or bored games (geddit)?

Or baking?

Or . . . beekeeping?

That's what former England captain **David Beckham** has decided to do with his spare, socially distanced time. Can you bee-lieve it? Away from his buzzy life in America – he owns a football team there, called Inter Miami – Becks settled down at his home in the English countryside, built himself a hive (the 'Flow Hive Classic 7 Frame', in case you wondered), and started making his own honey. Even in a big protective bodysuit, he still looks very stylish, and he's got his whole family helping out with his new passion project. How sweet!

As well as a nice way to connect with nature, beekeeping is also great for the environment. Bees play a very important part in the ecosystem because they transfer pollen between plants and so help flowers, fruits and vegetables to grow. Without bees, we wouldn't have so many of the lovely things we like to eat, so well done Becks for giving them a good home and looking after them so well! Plus, I bet they're great at bee-kicks now ...

Anyway, he has got such a buzz out of his new hobby (last pun, I promise!) that apparently he is now planning to start his own organic honey business. It'll probably be pretty expensive stuff, so my advice to Becks would be to buy Barnet Football Club next. Why? Because surely 'The Bees' would sell lots of his honey at their stadium, The Hive.

HOW YOU TOO CAN CHANGE THE WORLD

RECYCLE!

Most of the plastic, paper and glass that we use can be recycled and turned into something new, like an Adidas x Parley for the Oceans shirt, for example.

REUSE!

Instead of buying new bottles of water every time you need a drink, why not keep using the same one? That way, you'll use a lot less plastic like Héctor Bellerín.

SAVE WATER AND ELECTRICITY!

Even small changes can make a big difference, such as taking slightly shorter showers, or turning the tap off while you're cleaning your teeth. And if you're the last person to leave a room, remember to turn off the light.

WALK AND CYCLE!

If possible, try to find green ways to get to your football training and matches, and to go and watch your favourite team in action too. If it's too far away to walk or cycle, perhaps you could take public transport instead, or share a car with a couple of your friends or teammates like the Forest Green Rovers players do?

JOIN THE FOOTBALL4CLIMATE FAN CLUB AND TAKE PART IN PLANET SUPER LEAGUE!

Go to football4climate.org/fanclub and psl.football – get involved and protect the planet!

CHAPTER FIVE

FOOTBALL FOR A BRIGHTER FUTURE

'JJ', The Remarkable Referee Telling Girls to 'Play On!'

So far in this book, we've looked at lots of heroes who in their different ways have helped to make the world a better place and football a better game. They all have one thing in common, though – they're professional players (well, except Gandhi, but he's still really famous!). Superstars always get the glory, but there are lots of other individuals and organisations who are assisting and inspiring the next generation. And this section of stories is dedicated to them.

First up, we have **Jawahir Roble**, or 'JJ' as she is often called. She's the UK's first female Muslim referee and her aim is to encourage more girls to get involved in all areas of football – refereeing and coaching, as well as playing. But while more and more girls now dream of becoming 'the next Steph Houghton', not many seem to dream of becoming 'the next Sian Massey-Ellis', currently the Premier League's only female official. Massey-Ellis made her debut way back in 2010, and since then, no one has followed in her flag-waves, although watch out for Rebecca Welch, who in April 2021 became the first female referee in English Football League history.

And watch out for JJ too, of course! To be honest, though, she didn't always aim to be a referee. For a long time, she wanted to become a footballer instead. She first fell in love with the game as a kid growing up in Somalia, an African country with lots of forests, waterfalls and tropical grasslands (called savannas), which are home to wildlife including giraffes, elephants and the world's largest population of camels. Oh, and sitting on the east coast of Africa (known as 'The Horn'), Somalia also has lots of beautiful beaches too. It was there that JJ used to spend most of her time, kicking a ball around for hours with her friends until it got too dark to play. I don't know about you, but that sounds like the best day ever to me!

Unfortunately, however, the fun times didn't last.

A terrible civil war forced JJ and her family to flee to England when she was only ten years old. At first, she really missed her old life in Somalia, but there was one positive thing about her new home because where did she end up living? Wembley, the Home of Football! Whenever JJ played in the local park with her friends, she could see the national stadium in the distance and, if it was a matchday, she could hear the crowd too. It was so inspiring – perhaps one day when she became a famous footballer, she would get to perform there! Her parents, however, wanted her to study rather than play a sport that they thought was 'a man's game', so in the end JJ found a different path to pursue her passion.

'I DON'T SEE MYSELF AS A MUSLIM GIRL OR A FEMALE, I JUST SEE MYSELF SOMEONE WHO ACTUALLY LOVES FOOTBALL.'

One day in 2012, she went along to watch a football match where the teams waited and waited but still the referee didn't show up. What were they going to do? Without a match official, the game couldn't go on! What would you do in that situation – say 'I'll do it!' or stay quiet? Fortunately, JJ bravely agreed to step in and start her new career as a football referee. It wasn't just a walk around the pitch, though; no, suddenly she had so many important decisions to make:

Foul or play on? Penalty or dive? Yellow card or red?

Wow, JJ quickly realised that refereeing was a big responsibility, but an amazing adrenaline rush too! By the time she blew the final whistle, she had found her new favourite activity and her future career. She enjoyed the experience so much that she quickly got her FA qualifications and now she referees both men and women up to five times a day in the lower leagues of English football.

'No way, ref – you don't know what you're doing!'

It's hard work and JJ's journey hasn't been easy. A referee's job is already tough enough – making big decisions and dealing with really competitive players and spectators all the time – but she has had to overcome extra obstacles and discrimination as a black Muslim woman who wears a hijab (a religious head covering) on the pitch. Fortunately, JJ is a strong, confident character, and she's too positive and passionate about football to let anyone or anything stop her: 'If they do cross the line and say things like, "You're a girl, you shouldn't be in this game", then I try to educate them.'

Plus, she loves to prove people wrong: 'Players expect your typical-looking, middle-aged white man, not someone like me because they assume that I won't get the job done.' But she does, game after game, keeping calm and always in control. Her dream now is to one day referee in the Premier League, the Women's Super League, and even to follow in the footsteps of Stéphanie Frappart by taking charge of a Champions League match. Oh, and refereeing at Wembley Stadium would be really nice too!

But as well as her own personal ambitions, JJ also wants to be a role model for the next generation. She hopes to show that football 'is anyone's game', not just for men. 'I want to inspire as many young girls as possible,' she says. 'I'm a female and I'm gonna make sure more and more females get involved.' That's why she works with Football Beyond Borders and the Jason Roberts Foundation, two charities which offer education and coaching to disadvantaged kids in London. And when there are football games going on, it's always good to have a referee around!

JJ also uses her whistle and her organisational skills as a football coach. After finishing a degree in coaching, she decided to test her skills by starting a new team in her local neighbourhood, featuring seven of her nieces: 'Not a lot of kids in my area are playing football, especially girls. So, I wanted to change that and set up a girls' team. Then, I want to set up another girls' team, and then another. And then we have this area poppin'. That's the dream.'

Just in case JJ's story hasn't already inspired you to follow your passion for football and explore different areas of the game, she has a final message to send to you, so listen up:

**'WHEN NO ONE HAD MY BACK, I DID.
WHEN NO ONE BELIEVED IN ME, I DID.
WHEN NO ONE CHEERED FOR ME, I DID.
IN LIFE, IT CAN BE DIFFICULT TO FIND PEOPLE WHO SHARE YOUR VALUES AND YOUR**

MINDSET. UNTIL YOU FIND THEM, KEEP IT MOVING AND LOOK AFTER YOURSELF. WHEN YOU FIND THEM, KEEP THEM.

SURROUND YOURSELF WITH POSITIVE AND SUPPORTIVE PEOPLE.'

Equal Playing Field: Football's Record Breakers

When you've got an important message to share, what's the best way to make yourself heard? Some organisations create their own eye-catching social media content, while others ask famous stars to use their powerful voices. But the charity **Equal Playing Field** likes to do things slightly differently – it spreads the word by breaking world records.

The organisation was set up by a group of football-loving women who were frustrated at the way female sport was still treated differently all over the world. Women and girls had to overcome so many obstacles just to do what they loved, and they also received a lot less funding, lower wages and a lot less TV coverage too. What they wanted was an equal playing field:

'OPPORTUNITY, EQUALITY, RESPECT. NOTHING MORE, NOTHING LESS.'

But what could they do to help achieve that goal? They decided that they needed to do something big, something that would attract lots of attention. That's when one of the co-founders, Laura Youngson, had an incredible idea:

'IF WE CLIMB MANY MOUNTAINS EVERY SINGLE DAY JUST TO PLAY THE GAME WE LOVE, WHY NOT CLIMB ONE BIG ONE AND BANG A DRUM WHILST DOING SO?'

So, in June 2017, two teams of 15 female athletes, aged 15 to 55, and from over 20 different countries, spent a week climbing Mount Kilimanjaro in Tanzania, Africa's highest peak. That was only their first tough challenge, though. Once they got to the top, they set up the full-sized goals that they had carried all the way up the mountain, turned their walking poles into corner flags, marked out the lines with flour, and then played a proper 90-minute game on a pitch made of volcanic ash.

Talk about high drama (geddit?)! The teams featured recently retired international footballers like the USA's Lori Lindsey and France's Sandrine Dusang, but even they found it hard to show off their skills with so little oxygen in the air to breathe.

In the end, the game finished 0–0, but there were big celebrations at the final whistle, with tired players sinking to their knees in the ash. Together, the two teams of women had just set a new world record for the highest altitude football match ever! And when their epic achievement was reported on TV and in newspapers all over the world, it helped to raise lots of awareness about the fight for equality in women's sport.

'This is just the start,' one of the co-founders, Erin Blankenship, declared afterwards. 'We want every girl to have the opportunity to play this great game and we are excited about what the Equal Playing Field initiative achieves next.'

The answer was: breaking another world record, this time for the lowest altitude football match ever. For this challenge in 2018, they moved from the mountain to the sea. The two teams, featuring women from over 27 different countries, trekked 60 miles to a salt lake called the Dead Sea in the Middle Eastern country of Jordan. Along the way, they played games in four different cities and ran football camps to give opportunities to local girls who had never kicked a ball before. Then, once 'The Jordan Quest' arrived at the Dead Sea, it was time for the main event: the record-breaking football match.

This time, the players had the desert heat to deal with, but there was a lot more oxygen in the air for them to breathe, which meant more entertainment and more goals for the spectators to enjoy. Yes, 2,000 people turned up to watch, including Prince Ali bin Hussein of Jordan, and 500,000 more watched the video highlights all around the world. Equal Playing Field was certainly achieving their aim of attracting lots of attention!

Now that they had conquered the mountain

and the sea, what next? Well, to tie in with the 2019 Women's World Cup, they decided to try to break two more world records at one big Equal Playing Field 'Festival of Football'.

From Thursday 27 June through to Monday 1 July, the organisation took over the Olympic Lyonnaise Training Academy in France to play the world's largest five-a-side football match ever. The game went on for 69 hours, through day and night, and by the end, a record total of 822 players had been involved, aged 3 all the way up to 60, even including a group of British MPs! The final score was 400–369 to the red team, just in case you care about that ...

And with one new world record already set, why not break another for the most nationalities in an 11-a-side football match ever? Thankfully, this game was slightly shorter and smaller – it lasted less than 3 hours, with 114 players from 53 different countries!

While Equal Playing Field are really proud of the four world records, the main focus of all the charity's work is to create a better future for women and girls in sport. As another co-founder, Maggie Murphy, explains, 'We feel that our first World Record [climbing Mount Kilimanjaro] was about demanding respect from people who constantly try to put challenges in the paths of female footballers. The Jordan Quest was about opening the door and widening opportunity to girls less fortunate than some of us.' And the Festival of Football? That was about bringing women together from all over the world to talk, learn and play. 'We also hope to inspire them to take action for others. So that might be to set up the girls' team in the local school or help out with coaching at a local club.'

What amazing feat do you think they should attempt for their fifth world record – the first football game in the Arctic? Longest-ever Mexican wave? Most red cards in one match? Most keepie-uppies with a Brussels sprout? As we already know, the epic heroes at Equal Playing Field are up for any challenge.

Welcome to the Street Child World Cup!

Here's a tricky football quiz question for you – what do India, Tanzania, Brazil and Uzbekistan all have in common?

I'll give bonus points to any geography fans who said 'They've all got green on their national flags', but the correct football answer is ... they've all won the **Street Child World Cup!**

Just in case you haven't heard of this incredible competition before, let me give you the backstory. Workers at a UK charity called Amos Trust came up with the idea when they travelled to South Africa ahead of the 2010 FIFA World Cup. During their time in the city of Durban, they visited Umthombo, a local organisation which supports vulnerable children who, due to reasons such as poverty, discrimination and family violence, are homeless and have no option but to live on the streets.

Life for these young people was already very hard, but the local government was making things a lot worse. With the World Cup coming soon, the police were trying to 'clean up' the city by taking the street children away, as if they were no better than bits of litter. But that was illegal! When they heard about this horrible treatment, Amos Trust were determined to help. Millions of children – in South Africa, but also all over the world – were being denied their basic human rights to a safe home, good health and an education.

So, what could Amos Trust do to change the way homeless children were treated? What if they organised a big international event to give these young people a voice and a platform to share their experiences with each other and the world? And to make it really fun, what if they all played football, everyone's favourite sport? They could call it ... the Street Child World Cup! What do you think – one of the greatest ideas ever? It's so good that I bet that football genius we learned about earlier, Sam Weller Widdowson, wished he had come up with it.

The organisers quickly sorted out some simple rules for the tournament: each team had to feature a mix of boys and girls aged 14–16, who all had experience of living full-time on the streets without family. And after spreading the news far and wide, eight countries signed up to compete in the very first tournament in 2010.

From Africa: Tanzania and the hosts South Africa

From Asia: India, Philippines and Vietnam

From Central America: Nicaragua

And from Europe: Ukraine and England

Travelling to the tournament was the first challenge because many of the players didn't have passports or birth certificates. And without a proper place to call home, it was very hard for them to register for new identity documents. However, in the end, each team managed to overcome that obstacle and make it to South Africa for the first-ever Street Child World Cup.

'PEOPLE NORMALLY LOOK AT STREET CHILDREN AND THINK THEY CAN DO NOTHING

... BUT THIS TOURNAMENT WILL SHOW THAT WE CAN DO AMAZING THINGS.'

– Dennis David, from Tanzania

The exciting seven-a-side matches were held in the evenings at Durban University's indoor centre and, during the days, the kids went to the beach, to a safari park, and spent time at local schools, learning about each other and sharing stories and ideas through art and football. Sounds like the best trip ever, doesn't it? Thinking ahead to the future, each country's team even came up with their own manifesto, a list of changes they'd like their government to make, as well as changes they'd like to make themselves. They also then teamed up to write one united statement together:

'WE, THE CHILDREN OF THE STREET CHILD WORLD CUP SAY:
LISTEN TO US: WE HAVE THE RIGHT TO BE HEARD.
LISTEN TO US: HOME MEANS FAMILY. WE DO

NOT WANT TO STAY ON THE STREETS.
LISTEN TO US: WHEN WE SAY WE ARE ABUSED.
WE HAVE THE RIGHT TO BE PROTECTED.
LISTEN TO US: SO THAT WE CAN HAVE A FUTURE.'

– The Durban Street Child Declaration, presented to the UN Committee on Human Rights, 9 March 2011

Brilliant stuff, but I suppose you want to know who won the football tournament, don't you? The first-ever Street Child Champions of the World were ... India, who beat Tanzania 1–0 in the final. But really, they were all winners! The tournament had been a huge success and a really empowering experience for the kids. They returned to their countries feeling less lonely and helpless, and more determined to fight for their rights.

So, four years later, the second Street Child World Cup took place in Rio de Janeiro, Brazil, and this time it was even bigger. There were 230 children involved from 19 different countries, with separate tournaments for boys and girls. Tanzania beat their African neighbours Burundi 3–1 in the boys' final, while the hosts Brazil lifted the girls' trophy with a 1–0 win over the Philippines.

Once again, football was helping to bring young people together to fight for a better future. The Street Child World Cup was raising an important issue and spreading a very powerful message – everyone deserves to be treated equally. Famous people were listening and passing it on. Pope Francis blessed the tournament, Prince William sent a message of support to the teams, and Brazilian football legends Zico, Bebeto and Gilberto Silva all came along to watch. And most importantly, governments around the world were starting to make changes to better protect their most vulnerable children.

In 2018, the Street Child World Cup moved on to Moscow, Russia. The matches took place at Lokomotiv Moscow's 27,000-seater stadium, with the Uzbekistan boys and Brazil girls crowned champions. And away from the pitch, one player from each of the 23 teams stood up and gave a speech about the problems for street children in their country, and what football can do to help. They're all fantastic, but this one by Hendra from the Philippines is my favourite:

> **'WE ARE THE AVENGERS. WHY AVENGERS? BECAUSE WE HAVE FACED MANY CHALLENGES AND OBSTACLES IN OUR LIVES. BUT STILL WE CONTINUE TO WALK THE PATH TOWARDS OUR FUTURE.**
>
> **WE DIDN'T EXPECT TO BE HERE AND REPRESENT OUR COUNTRY AT THIS EVENT. EVEN THOUGH WE ARE STREET CHILDREN WE LEARN TO VALUE EACH OTHER AND TAKE CARE OF EACH OTHER BECAUSE WE BELIEVE THAT WHEN WE SHOW WE CARE, EVERYBODY WINS.'**

The Supergoats Who Fell in Love with Football

With the right opportunities to learn and grow, it's amazing what young people can achieve. In most societies, that's why we go to school, but that option isn't always available. In Jharkhand, for example, a rural region in the east of India with lots of rice fields and farms growing vegetables, only 50 per cent of young girls go to school and only 45 per cent are able to read, because of problems such as poverty, gender inequality, violence and child marriage. So, an organisation called **Yuwa** set out to empower the girls of Jharkhand, giving them a different kind of education and a brighter future. And what did they use? Football!

Yuwa (which means 'youth' in Hindi, the local language) was started by an American teacher called Franz Gastler in 2009. When he arrived in the town of Ormanjhi, he was struck by the inequality he saw around him – 'the boys all go out to play, while the girls work'. Girls were expected to stay at home and help their mothers with the cooking and cleaning, but that wasn't fair. Why shouldn't they have fun too? So, Gastler asked his students what they'd like to play, and they all said football. Football? Gastler knew a lot about skiing and ice hockey, but not 'soccer', as Americans call it. Oh well, he would just have to learn the basics quickly by watching online videos.

'How often do you want to play?' he asked, and the girls answered straight away:

'Every day!' (Well, obviously – what a silly question!)

'And what do you need to play?'

'A place to play, a ball and a coach.'

Seeing how passionate the local girls were, Gastler had a great idea – to use football as a tool for education. Yuwa was born, and from that first team of 12 players, the organisation grew and grew. The girls would wake up at 4 a.m. each day because that's how eager they were to fit as much learning and playing into every

single day! Can you match that passion? Which would you choose – an extra hour of sport or an extra hour of sleep? No, dreaming about football doesn't count …

Before their regular school started, the girls would come to Yuwa for extra English, Maths and Science classes, and then after school and after helping their families with the housework, they returned for football practice. The girls had lots of fun out on the field, while also building their self-confidence and self-worth. They began to believe in a better, brighter future for themselves, where they could go to university and get good jobs, rather than be forced into marriage at a young age.

Yuwa was an instant success, and especially when it came to sport. The girls worked so hard to develop the football skills to go with their togetherness and fighting spirit that, within months, 13 of the players had made it into Jharkhand's state teams. Two years and many wins later (against boys as well as girls!), three of them were even called up to India's Under-14 national squad.

Football really was helping to change the lives of the Yuwa girls, and it even gave them the opportunity to visit other countries. In 2013, the team were invited to travel to Spain and play in two important international youth tournaments. First, they went to San Sebastián to compete in the Donosti Cup against 35 other teams from around the world. For the girls, it was the first time they had ever seen the sea, let alone swam in it, and it was also the first time they had ever worn proper football boots. Back home in India, they usually just played barefoot, but this was the big time now. At the opening ceremony, they walked around Real Sociedad's Anoeta Stadium in their sarees in front of thousands of supporters, while fireworks exploded in the sky.

Despite all these exciting new experiences, however, the girls stayed focused on football. They were there to win, to make their community proud, and on the team bus, they all sang together:

'We are young, so special; we are on the ball, we attack the net; all hail Yuwa!'

Before each game kicked off, the players formed a tight team circle in the centre of the pitch. After a few words from their captain, Neeta Kumari, they raised their arms in the air and chanted as one: 'Yuwa! Yuwa!'

With their skills, smiles and fun goal celebrations, the girls in green soon became everyone's favourite football team. Yuwa won two out of their three group matches before losing in the quarter-finals. Not bad at all, and there was even better to come at the Gasteiz Cup a week later. There, they finished third out of ten teams to take the bronze medal, with two wins, two losses and one draw. What an achievement! The girls from Jharkhand returned home as heroes. 'We were treated like princes everywhere we went,' said Neeta.

Soon, the famous 'Yuwa Supergoats', as they were now called, were setting off on another international football adventure: to Minnesota – the American state where Gastler grew up – to become the first Indian team ever to play in the Schwan's USA Cup. It was a huge competition and the girls had never played on grass pitches before, but they battled hard, drawing three matches before being knocked out in the play-offs.

Never mind, for the Supergoats, their football journey was about so much more than winning. They returned to Spain to compete in the Donosti Cup in 2016 and 2018, and then in 2019, four of the girls – Neeta, Hema, Konika and Radha Kumari – took a trip to Monaco, but this time not to play in a tournament. Instead, they were there to collect a very special prize, the Laureus Sport for Good Award. At the fancy ceremony, famous stars including tennis player Novak Djokovic and football manager Arsène Wenger clapped and cheered as the Yuwa players made their way up on stage. Gastler spoke first but then he handed the microphone to Radha, who stole the show with her courage, passion, and her positive message:

'YUWA HAS CHANGED ME. YUWA GAVE ME THE CONFIDENCE TO STAND IN FRONT OF YOU ALL AND IT GAVE ME THE ENCOURAGEMENT TO PROCEED FORWARD IN MY LIFE, NO MATTER WHAT OBSTACLES I FACE . . . I WANT TO KEEP GOING FORWARD AND ENCOURAGE ALL THE GIRLS BACK IN JHARKHAND TO EXPLORE THINGS AND TRY. IT WILL GET YOU SOMEWHERE.'

'I WILL GO MY OWN WAY. AND I REALLY HOPE THAT MANY GIRLS WILL FOLLOW IN MY FOOTSTEPS, IN LINE WITH THE MOTTO: IF SHE CAN DO IT, SO CAN I.'

– Neeta Kumari, Yuwa captain, 2013

Good Guys vs Bad Bankers – A Football Match with a Message

On Saturday 5 September, 2020, a very special football game took place in London. No, not Arsenal vs Aston Villa, or West Ham vs Bournemouth; I'm talking about Extinction Rebellion vs Sharklays. Who? What? Where?

It was played all over London, actually, including in Trafalgar Square and outside a branch of Barclays bank in Piccadilly Circus. 'What, a moving football match?' you're probably wondering. 'How does that work?' Right, I should really explain a little more about the two teams involved.

At one end, wearing football kits under bright orange bibs … **EXTINCTION REBELLION!** 'XR' is a global environmental movement which calls for governments to take action on climate change.

And at the other end, wearing suits and ties ... **SHARKLAYS!** They're a team of XR members who are pretending to be bankers and businessmen from oil and gas companies like BP and ExxonMobil, as well as banks like Barclays. According to XR, they're the bad guys (Sharklays, geddit? A bit harsh on sharks, if you ask me ...). Why?

Well, you might know Barclays as the official banking partner of the English Premier League, but the problem is they also make lots of their money from fossil fuels. As we learned in the 'Protecting the Planet' section, fossil fuels are really bad for the environment, and that's why XR decided to use a football match to fight back and tell their side of the story.

So, do you want to hear what happened on the pitch? Well, it started off as a good, fair game until the baddie bankers decided to change the rules and move the goalposts. Boooo! 'Come on, ref, do something – they're cheating!' you're hopefully shouting at this point. But sorry, that won't work because, once they'd bribed him with lots of money, the referee was on the Sharklays team too, helping them to win!

It was XR's clever way of showing that it's an unfair playing field, and that we, just like the referee should have done, need to stand up and show the red card to the big, rich banks and companies who are still buying and selling fossil fuels.

But what about you? Which football team would you play for – Extinction Rebellion or Sharklays?

By losing their match in London to show how unfair things are, Extinction Rebellion are hoping to win the bigger battle going on all over the world, for the future of football and for the future of our planet.

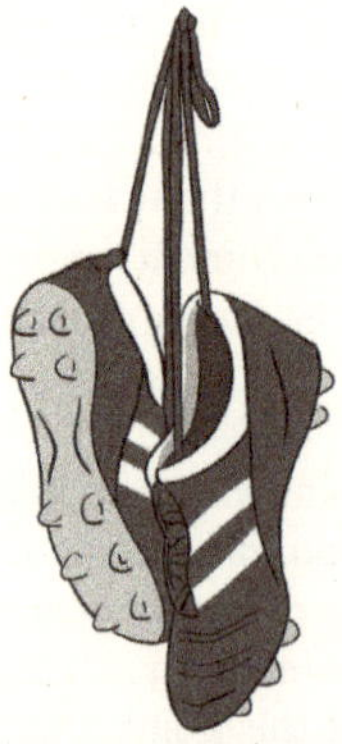

PASS YOUR FOOTBALL PASSION ON TO OTHER KIDS

Whenever you're around younger members of your family, or younger age groups at school or your football club, always be encouraging and help them to enjoy the game too. You could even give coaching a go!

EXPLORE EVERY AREA OF FOOTBALL

Remember, there are lots of different ways to make your mark on the game. Who knows, you might end up becoming a physio, or a referee, just like JJ!

SHOW YOUR SUPPORT FOR ALL THE AMAZING FOOTBALL ORGANISATIONS

Tell your friends about the Street Child World Cup, for example, help fundraise for your country, and then cheer on all the teams at the next tournament in Qatar in 2022!

- **MAKE YOUR OWN MANIFESTO, LIKE THE KIDS AT THE STREET CHILD WORLD CUP**

  Try writing down a list of the Top 5 things you'd like to change about your country. Then, once you've finished, why not share your ideas with your class at school?

- **AND IF THE STORY OF EQUAL PLAYING FIELD HAS INSPIRED YOU, SEE IF YOU CAN SET SOME NEW WORLD RECORDS TOO!**

CHAPTER SIX

INCREDIBLE KIDS

Panyee Football Club and Their Fantastic Floating Pitch

Football is a simple game and that's one of the many, many reasons why it's the world's most popular sport. Yes, the latest boots would be nice and so would your favourite club's new kit, but you don't need any of that fancy equipment. All you need is a ball, a few friends, objects for goalposts – jumpers, rocks, trees, anything! – and a place to play.

That does sound simple, but what if you don't have a local park or pitch? Well, in some places, people play in the streets instead, or on the beach if they live by the sea. The kids at **Panyee Football Club**, however, came up with an even better idea: they built themselves a floating football pitch!

Panyee FC are a team from a tiny fishing village called Ko Panyi, in Thailand, a country in South East Asia famous for its yummy street food, tropical beaches and beautiful old Buddhist temples. The population of Ko Panyi is less than 2,000 people but, as you're about to see, they're really passionate about football.

It all started way back in 1986, when they first fell in love with the World Cup. Mexico 86 – what a tournament! Before you ask, no, I'm not old enough to remember it. In fact, I hadn't even been born, but I've heard all about it: Gary Lineker of England, Rudi Völler of West Germany, Careca of Brazil, and the star of the whole show, Diego Maradona, who led Argentina all the way to the trophy. It was incredible to watch, and the people of Ko Panyi got to see it all on TV.

The local kids were so inspired that they decided to form their own football team: Panyee Football Club. They all wanted to be the next Maradona now! No, the Thailand national team had never qualified for the World Cup before, but they dared to dream. Maybe they could be the football heroes who finally made their country proud. There was just one problem with their plan, though: Panyee FC had nowhere to play.

To make it easy for the fishermen, their whole village had been built on stilts above the water. They called it 'The Floating Island'. There was just enough space for the mosque, the school, and all the shops and houses, but an extra sports field? No way!

It looked like the local kids might have to give up on their World Cup dream, until one of them had an incredible idea:

'WHY DON'T WE BUILD A PITCH ON WATER?'

They already lived on a floating island, so why not play on a floating football pitch too? Perfect!

Most of the adults thought it was a ridiculous plan that would never work, but the kids were so determined (and football-mad) that they carried on anyway. They went around Ko Panyi collecting up every bit of spare wood they could find, from houses and fishing boats and rafts. Then, they set to work after school each day, putting it all together to form a football pitch. It wasn't that big, or

steady, or safe when the surface got slippery and wet, but the most important thing was that it was theirs and they were free to play their favourite sport. Little did they know, that pitch would go on to change their lives and their floating island forever.

At first, the ball fell into the water all the time, and each time, the player who kicked it would have to jump in and get it. But the more Panyee FC practised, the better they became at keeping the ball on the pitch and under control. In fact, they were improving in every way – passing, tackling, dribbling and shooting. So, when they saw a poster for a tournament called the Pangha Cup, they decided they were ready to take the next step and compete against teams from the mainland.

'Good luck!' the rest of the village cheered as Panyee FC set off on their first football adventure. The local people were so impressed with their young players that they had paid for new kits and boots. 'Go make us proud!'

And they did. Playing on proper football pitches that didn't sway with the sea? No problem! The Panyee FC players were now so skilful that they made it all the way to the semi-finals. There, however, they came up against a really good team, plus some really bad weather. By half-time, they were 2–0 down and their boots were heavy with rainwater. What could they do to turn things around?

It looked like their Pangha Cup journey might be over, until one of them had another incredible idea:

'WHY DON'T WE GO BACK TO PLAYING BAREFOOT, LIKE WE USUALLY DO AT HOME?'

With their boots off, they were so much better! Panyee FC scored two goals to make it 2–2 but, sadly, it was their opponents who got the last-minute winner.

Oh well, they had done really well to get so far, and the players returned home as heroes. From now on, football would be Ko Panyi's favourite sport forever! The village built a new, bigger and better floating pitch, where more people could play, and the ball would hardly ever fall into the water. It was perfect; there were no nails sticking out in random places, and it even had proper full-sized goals!

With a better pitch, Panyee FC were able to produce even better players, especially with those football-crazy kids who had built the original in 1986 now working as the coaches. Between 2004 and 2010, the club were crowned the Youth Champions of Southern Thailand for seven years in a row. So far, none of their players have yet gone on to represent the national team but a few have become professionals in the Thai football league.

So, there you have it, the story of how an incredible

team of kids and their floating pitch helped to change a community forever. Not only has football brought the people of Ko Panyi together and given them a fun new game to play, but it has also brought tourism and money to what is a very poor part of the world. Because what football fan wouldn't want to visit the home of the mighty Panyee FC, and hopefully have a kickaround on their famous floating pitch?

The Keepie-uppie Queen of COVID-19

Keepie-uppies – we can all do a few, can't we, but what's your record? Ten? Twenty? Fifty? What about 7.1 million?

That's the ambitious target that one 11-year-old set for herself in March 2020 – one keepie-uppie for each of the key workers playing their part in protecting the UK during the COVID-19 pandemic. For football fan **Imogen Papworth-Heidel**, whose parents both work for the NHS, it was a way of saying thanks and hopefully raising some money for charity while, at the same time, keeping herself busy in the back garden during the boring national lockdown.

It was a fantastic idea, but wasn't it a football mission impossible? Imogen is a talented player who trains with her local club, Cambridge United, but she soon realised that even she couldn't make it all the way to 7.1 million on her own. 'My original target was 200 keepie-uppies a day,' she said, 'and it was going to take me 97 years to do.'

Ninetey-seven years! That meant Imogen would have to keep up her keepie-uppies until the age of 108, which would make her even older than Captain Tom Moore, the hero who had inspired her by walking a hundred laps around his garden before his hundredth birthday.

No, there had to be a better – and faster – way to achieve her goal. So, Imogen upped her daily target from 200 to 2,000, and decided to turn it into a big team effort, just like football. When she asked others to help her by 'donating' keepie-uppies, over 2,000 sports clubs, school groups and individuals responded:

- The Cambridge United manager, Mark Bonner, loved the idea and got all of his players involved too.
- People sent in videos from all over the world, including one patient recovering from cancer who did keepie-uppies with a balloon next to her hospital bed.
- England players Lucy Bronze and Marcus

Rashford also offered their support, as well as their football skills.

As word spread far and wide about her amazing challenge, Imogen received over 50 videos a day. Her poor parents went through each and every one, counting the keepie-uppies and adding them to the total. Full marks for effort and for the maths skills!

But let's get back to Imogen, the true hero of this story. For 195 days in a row, she went out to her back garden and juggled the football for hours, even when the weather was cold and horrible. It was an incredible

effort, and she was helping to inspire others too. In July 2020, the English FA announced a special 'Lionhearts' squad, 'to recognise 23 individuals who have gone above and beyond during the COVID-19 crisis to celebrate their efforts and thank them for everything they've done'.

The team leader? Captain Tom, of course!

And wearing the Number 7 shirt, once worn by David Beckham, was . . . Imogen!

She was even invited to go to St George's Park, the training centre for England football teams, where she met two of her heroes, Lionesses Georgia Stanway and Izzy Christiansen. When they heard all about Imogen's keepie-uppie challenge and how close she was to reaching her target – only 50,000 to go! – they helped her out with a few more, and so did fellow England stars like Declan Rice, Trent Alexander-Arnold, Fran Kirby, Kieran Trippier, Mason Mount and Tammy Abraham.

Another 836 keepie-uppies to add to the total! The finish line was in sight, and with just 3,000 to go, Imogen moved her skills show to the pitch at Cambridge United's Abbey Stadium.

. . . 7,099,997 . . . 7,099,998 . . . 7,099,999 . . . 7,100,000!

As she booted the ball high into the air, Imogen raised her arms above her head like a champion. In total, she had completed 1,123,586 keepie-uppies all by herself. Sadly, there was no crowd there cheering for her, but what an achievement – instead of 97 years, it had only taken six-and-a-half months, and instead of the £1,300 she hoped to raise for charity, she raised over £13,000!

'I'M JUST ABSOLUTELY SPEECHLESS AT HOW MUCH MONEY WE'VE RAISED, HOW MANY KEEPIE-UPPIES HAVE BEEN DONATED AND HOW MANY KIND MESSAGES OF SUPPORT HAVE COME IN.'

At a time of great hardship and suffering, Imogen and her keepie-uppie challenge had really helped to lift the nation's spirits, while also encouraging people of all ages to grab a football, get involved and stay active.

Alfie, the Humble Hero of Anfield

From keepie-uppies to pocket money – here's another story about the kindness of a young football fan. In 2018, **Alfie Radford** was only seven years old when he went to watch Liverpool play Porto in the Champions League at Anfield with his dad, Tom.

Lucky boy, eh, and he had even saved up £10 of his pocket money. So, was Alfie going to spend it on something nice at the Liverpool club shop? No, on the way to the game, he asked to stop at a supermarket instead.

'Oh, the boy wants to buy some sweets!' you might well be thinking, but guess again.

What Alfie did next was amazing – he used his pocket money to fill a bag with £10 worth of tinned food, which he then carried to the stadium to donate to Fans Supporting Foodbanks, a charity set up by both Liverpool and Everton fans to support less fortunate families in the local area. What a little legend!

'Why did you do it?' a TV reporter asked him a few days later.

'To save some people's lives,' Alfie replied. He knew that there were children his own age in Liverpool who were hungry, and he wanted to help.

And that's just the first half of this heart-warming story. Fans Supporting Foodbanks gave Alfie their 'Fan of the Month' award, posting a picture on social media with the words:

'THE FUTURE OF OUR CITY & THE BEAUTIFUL GAME IS SAFE IF WE PRODUCE CHILDREN LIKE ALFIE RADFORD.'

The story soon spread until it reached Liverpool's left-back, Andrew Robertson, a big supporter of foodbanks ever since his early footballing days in Scotland. For his 21st birthday, he asked his friends and family to donate to a foodbank rather than buy him a present, and he also gave large amounts of money to six organisations in his hometown of Glasgow during the COVID-19 crisis in 2020.

So, when he heard what young Alfie had done, at the age of only seven, Robertson was so impressed that he decided to write him a letter to say thanks:

> *'Dear Alfie,*
>
> *It's Andy Robertson here from Liverpool.*
>
> *I saw on Twitter that you did something very special for the foodbanks at Anfield last night.*
>
> *I remember being your age just how important pocket money is and how there's hundreds of things you could have bought for yourself with it. For you to give that up for people who are having a tough time and need some help to get by is absolutely amazing.'*

Alfie was delighted and, as well as the letter, Robertson also gave him a signed Liverpool shirt, but not his own: 'Let's be honest Alfie – no-one wants the left back's shirt –

which is why I got you Bobby's [Firmino] instead.'

What a win, although I'd take Robbo's shirt any day!

Alfie's act of kindness had led to another, and when the letter went viral, it encouraged other football fans to donate to their local foodbanks too, raising lots more awareness about a very important issue.

Andy and Alfie – two of football's good guys for sure. One went on to lift the Champions League and the Premier League, and the other? Well, he's not even ten years old yet, but as Fans Supporting Foodbanks said, the future looks a lot brighter thanks to incredible kids like Alfie.

The Brilliant Young Players Who Are Passing the Football On

As Alfie's story shows, a single act of kindness can lead to many more. So, think about it – if we all did one random nice thing to help others every single day, imagine what we could achieve. We could create a cascade of kindness and truly change the world!

'A cascade?' I hear you ask. 'What's that?' It's a small waterfall, with a never-ending flow. But imagine that every drop of water was a generous act instead – how cool would that be?

Or, as this is a football book, maybe you'd rather think of it as a beautiful team move, where the ball (or kindness!) is passed on from player to player, from one end of the pitch to the other, until eventually the striker scores! Manchester City manager Pep Guardiola thinks that's the perfect goal and his team pulled it off in 2017, after an astonishing 52 passes! Leroy Sané was the one who finally put the ball in the net, but all 11 City stars had played their part, including the keeper.

So, what can we do to keep the kindness flowing just like Pep's pass-and-move football? The possibilities are endless, but here are a few examples to inspire you.

Remember everyone's favourite football team the Yuwa Supergoats from India, who you read about in 'Football for a Brighter Future'? Well, the original group of young footballers – the 'Class of 09' as I like to call them – are grown-ups now, but their incredible captain **Neeta** is still studying at Yuwa school, and she's also coaching her own girls' team in her local community. Yes, having experienced the power of football herself as a Supergoat, Neeta is now passing on her passion and skills to the next generation: 'I want to be an example to other girls, so that they can tell their family, "Wow, see that girl! She has done it, why can't I?"'

Yes, coaching is a great way for young football fans to give back to the game they love. In the USA, the national football federation runs a free after-school programme called Soccer for Success, which, like Yuwa, combines fun sports sessions with lessons in teamwork, confidence, respect and healthy living. It's a very popular programme and one boy, **Daniel**, enjoyed it so much that he didn't want it to end. He had learned so much during his time at Soccer for Success, so he asked if he could come back as a volunteer coach and mentor, to support and encourage more young footballers like him. After a few more years of dedication for free, Daniel achieved the qualifications he needed to get a paid job with the programme, and now he's one of the head coaches!

But if you don't fancy becoming 'the next Pep Guardiola', no problem – as you've seen throughout this book, football kindness comes in lots of different forms. Instead of coaching or mentoring, maybe you could raise money for charity like **Louis**? For his bar mitzvah (a religious Jewish ceremony that happens when a boy turns 13), he was asked to pick a project that would help make the world a better place. It didn't take him long to come up with an idea: give more kids the chance to play football! 'I love the game and wanted it to be passed on to kids who don't have the resources and money to play,' he said. So, Louis did lots of jobs like gardening and pet-sitting, and asked all his neighbours if they had any sports clothing that they didn't need any more. Three months later, he had collected nearly £200 to spend on new sports equipment, plus over 300 pieces of football kit (all washed and clean, I promise!).

So, have the stories of Neeta, Daniel and Louis inspired you to do something nice to help others? How would you like to pass your football passion on? You could do it through actions, or through words – an 'Unlucky, keep going!' for a teammate low in confidence, or a 'Great goal!' to a promising player in a younger age group. However you decide to help, you'll be keeping that cascade of kindness flowing.

The Cheeky Kid Who Pulled Off the Perfect Prank

How do you think you'd react if you were lucky enough to meet one of the greatest players in the world? Would you hug them and go all hyper, or get really shy and star-struck? Well, what if they played for a team which was one of your biggest rivals – would that make any difference?

Back in February 2006, **Jake Nickless** was a five-year-old Chelsea fan whose dream had just come true – as a birthday present, he was going to be a mascot for his club's massive Premier League match against Liverpool. How exciting! At the time, Chelsea were flying high at the top of the table, 12 points ahead of Manchester United in second place. The Blues were on track to win a second Premier League title in a row, but standing in their way were Liverpool, and in particular their captain and midfield maestro, Steven Gerrard.

Gerrard was 25 years old and at the peak of his powers as one of the best players in the world. Nine months earlier, he had led his team to Champions League glory and, three months later, he would lift the FA Cup too, after a win over West Ham that would become known as 'The Steven Gerrard Final'. So, if anyone was going to cause Chelsea trouble at Stamford Bridge, it was certainly Stevie G.

What could they do to stop him? Well, the manager, José Mourinho, set up his team with two defensive midfielders, Claude Makélélé and Michael Essien, to try to keep Gerrard quiet. But what he didn't know was that before kick-off, a cheeky little kid had already given them a helping hand.

In the tunnel, Jake stood with Chelsea captain John Terry, ready to play his part for the team. He had his hair dyed blue and his dad's plan in his head: 'If you see Gerrard, make sure you wind him up.' At last, the Liverpool captain appeared – this was Jake's big chance, but was he brave enough to go through with it?

Why not? With the TV cameras watching, he called, 'Gerrard!' and out went his little arm to offer a handshake. Stevie G,

being a nice guy, was happy to say hello back, but as he stretched out his arm, Jake pulled his hand away in a flash, and played the nose trumpet instead. *Nana nana na!*

It was the perfect playground prank to help put Gerrard off his game. Although he gave the boy a playful slap on the cheek, Jake had really got him good.

'The only time I smiled in the tunnel was when the Chelsea mascot played a trick on me,' Stevie admitted later in his autobiography.

Liverpool went on to lose the match 2–0, while Chelsea won the title by eight points. Well done, Jake! Not only had he helped his team to win the league, but his dad also bought him two new PlayStation games for pranking Stevie G so successfully.

Jake is now 21 years old and a player himself. He recently signed for Billericay Town, a club in the sixth tier of the English Football League. Apparently, he's an attacking midfielder with a good eye for goal – just like his old enemy, Stevie G!

HOW YOU TOO CAN CHANGE THE WORLD

FIGHT FOR THE RIGHT TO PLAY

Everyone should have a local football pitch near where they live, where it's free to play. If you don't, why not see if you can change that? Unless you've got building skills like Panyee FC, it might be safest to speak to your MP instead! Or you could create a petition and ask your friends to sign it and show their support.

USE YOUR FOOTBALL PASSION FOR GOOD

The possibilities are endless! You could enter a team in a charity tournament, volunteer at a fundraising event, donate your football shirts to charity when they get too small (like Louis), or …

COMPLETE A CHALLENGE FOR CHARITY

Why not set yourself an almost impossible task like Imogen and ask other people to sponsor you and get involved too? There are so many possibilities, but special shout-outs go to:

Milan Kumar, aged 8, who cycled around the Bolton Wanderers stadium 500 times and also published a book in aid of the National Literacy Trust.
Oliver Hedley, aged 7, who drew 30 pictures in 30 days to raise money for the children's charity KIND.
Alexander Plews, aged 9, who cut off all of his lovely long hair to support the diabetes charity JDRF (Gary Mabbutt must be particularly proud of him).

DON'T FORGET THOSE LESS FORTUNATE THAN YOU

Try to be as kind and understanding as Alfie, and if you do have a spare bit of pocket money, think about using it to help others in need.

SHARE ALL THE SKILLS YOU'VE LEARNED THROUGH FOOTBALL

Maybe you could mentor your friends and younger children, like Neeta and Daniel. You could teach them about dribbling and ball control, but also decision-making and co-operation. It's as important to be a good team player at school and with your family as it is on the pitch.

CONCLUSION

There goes the final whistle! Sadly, you've reached the end of this second collection of *Unbelievable Football* stories. I really hope you've enjoyed reading all about the important role that the game can play as a force for good in the world. As the amazing Nelson Mandela, former President of South Africa, put it in 2000:

'SPORT HAS THE POWER TO CHANGE THE WORLD. IT HAS THE POWER TO INSPIRE, IT HAS THE POWER TO UNITE PEOPLE IN A WAY THAT LITTLE ELSE DOES.'

Mandela was talking about all sports, but as you know by now, football is the most popular and the most powerful sport in the world! Just think back to all the remarkable stories that you've read in this book:

- The stars who have spoken out for social change.
- The kind footballers, past and present, who have shared their success with those less fortunate.
- The teams who have helped to bring divided countries together.
- The players and clubs who are working hard to protect our planet.
- The individuals and organisations who are inspiring the next generation to get involved in the game.
- The incredible kids, like you, who are carrying football forward towards a brighter future.

So, what are you waiting for?! Grab your ball, use your voice, and play your part. Feel inspired to make a difference, just like your football heroes, and set an example for others to follow. Be courageous and kind to all – both teammates and opponents, on and off the pitch. You already knew that the game could change your life, but now you know that it can change the whole world too.

Football – it's unbelievable, isn't it?

ACKNOWLEDGEMENTS

Unbelievable Football 2 – the difficult second season. Can we carry on fighting for top trophies and avoid becoming one-book wonders? Of course we can! But just to make sure we don't slip up like Stevie G, we've gone for an even bigger and better squad this time. So, I'd like to say a massive thank you to:

My editorial dream team: Julie Ferris, Victoria Walsh and Laura 'The Gaffer' Horsley

Illustrator extraordinaire: Ollie Mann

Director of Football: Nick Walters

Assistant Manager: Iona Symington

Team Mascot: Claude the Sausage Dog

New signings who played starring roles: Alice Devine, Tom Perez and the amazing Jawahir 'JJ' Roble

And most important of all . . .

The Supporters: family, friends, authors, teachers, booksellers, librarians and, of course, readers. This book, like football itself, would be nothing without the fans.

SOURCES

Marvellous Marcus Rashford and the Fight to End Food Poverty
Rashford, Marcus. Quote reproduced in 'Marcus Rashford: the making of a food superhero.' *Guardian*, 17 January 2021. www.theguardian.com/football/2021/jan/17/marcus-rashford-the-making-of-a-food-superhero-child-hunger-free-school-meals, accessed 11 May 2021.
Rashford, Marcus. Twitter.com. 15 June 2020. https://twitter.com/MarcusRashford/status/1272302819819823105, accessed 11 May 2021.
Rashford, Marcus. Twitter.com. 21 October 2020. https://twitter.com/MarcusRashford/status/1318980281999761408, accessed 11 May 2021.
Speaking Up
Sterling, Raheem. 'Raheem Sterling: I don't want the next generation to suffer like me.' *The Times*, 23 April 2019. www.thetimes.co.uk/article/raheem-sterling-i-dont-want-the-next-generation-to-suffer-like-me-5ng7tpqkq, accessed 11 May 2021.
Murphy, Jim. *The 10 Matches That Changed the World* (London: Biteback Publishing, 2014).
Canoville, Paul. *Black and Blue* (London: Headline, 2008).
The Skilful Scot Who Kicked Down Barriers
'Banned by Scotland, so Rose won the World Cup with Italy instead.' BBC.co.uk. www.bbc.co.uk/programmes/articles/1QZRzRJMZ4pyt9yRphyr8kt/banned-by-scotland-so-rose-won-the-world-cup-with-italy-instead, accessed 11 May 2021.
Storey, Daniel. 'Rose Reilly: The lost superstar of women's football.' iNews. www.inews.co.uk/sport/football/womens-football/rose-reilly-scotland-fa-football-reims-milan-lecce-best-womens-player-411226, accessed 11 May 2021.
'Rose Reilly.' BBC ALBA. 26 August 2020.
Equal Pay to Play: The Team Protest that Went Viral
'2020 FIFPRO Player Voice Award: Cyprus Women's Team fights for equality.' YouTube, FIFPRO. 18 February 2021. www.youtube.com/watch?v=zi5TPqWt_OQ, accessed 11 May 2021.
Mahatma Gandhi's Passive Resisters
'Mahatma Gandhi, football legend.' FIFA.com. 22 October 2021. www.fifa.com/news/mahatma-gandhi-football-legend-1322010, accecssed 11 May 2021.
Juan Mata, the Nicest Man in Football
Mata, Juan. Quoted in 'Juan Mata: "Footballers live in a bubble and earn an obscene amount of money".' Sports Mole. www.sportsmole.co.uk/football/man-utd/news/mata-footballers-live-in-a-bubble_271366.html, accessed 11 May 2021.
Mata, Juan. *Suddenly a Footballer* (London: Reach Sport, 2020).
The French Superstar Who Gave Away His World Cup Winnings
Mbappé, Kylian. Quote reproduced in 'Kylian Mbappé explains why he donated his $500,000 World Cup wage to charity.' Sport Bible. 11 October 2018. www.sportbible.com/football/news-take-a-bow-kylian-mbappe-explains-why-he-donated-world-cup-match-fees-to-charity-20181011, accessed 11 May 2021.

Football, Food and Friendship at the 1991 FIFA Women's World Cup
Theivam, Kieran & Kassouf, Jeff. *The Making of the Women's World Cup* (London: Robinson, 2019).
Hurray for the Lockdown Heroes!
Mabbutt, Gary. Quote reproduced in 'Tottenham legend Gary Mabbutt on his selfless lockdown phone calls.' *Telegraph*, 19 June 2020. www.telegraph.co.uk/lifestyle/donate-your-words/gary-mabbutt-lockdown-phone-calls/, accessed 11 May 2021.
Macari, Lou. Quotes reproduced in 'The former footballer who set up a homeless shelter: "I thought surely we can do better than this?".' BBC Radio 5 Live. www.bbc.co.uk/programmes/articles/1yNNxC7w0C1Dgc3vjZNtY9Y/the-former-footballer-who-set-up-a-homeless-shelter-i-thought-surely-we-can-do-better-than-this, accessed 11 May 2021.
Otorbaeva, Aidana. Quote reproduced in 'Gamechangers: Aidana Otorbaeva, a different type of football hero.' AFC. www.the-afc.com/news/afcsection/gamechangers-aidana-otorbaeva-a-different-type-of-football-hero-x3343, accessed 11 May 2021.
Predrag Pašić and the Ladybirds of Peace
'Football Rebels, Season 1 Episode 3: Predrag Pašić and the siege of Sarajevo.' Al Jazeera. 26 March 2013. www.aljazeera.com/program/football-rebels/2013/3/27/predrag-pasic-and-the-siege-of-sarajevo, accessed 11 May 2021.
Germany: Divided by Politics, (Re)United by Football
Klinsmann, Jürgen. Quoted reproduced in 'Germany's '96 harmony strikes chord for Klinsmann.' UEFA.com. www.uefa.com/uefaeuro-2020/news/0253-0d7da6abdace-07c473985042-1000--germany-s-96-harmony-strikes-chord-for-klinsmann/, accessed 11 May 2021.
Mende, Jens & Schwarz, Manuel. 'Sammer, Ballack and Kroos can't stop East German football fading.' DPA International. 7 November 2019. www.dpa-international.com/topic/sammer-ballack-kroos-can-t-stop-east-german-football-fading-urn%3Anewsml%3Adpa.com%3A20090101%3A191107-99-616567, accessed 11 May 2021.
Ronaldo, Ronaldinho, and the Match for Peace
Ronaldo. Quote reproduced in 'Brazil and Haiti play for peace.' Al Jazeera, 18 August 2014. www.aljazeera.com/news/2004/8/18/brazil-and-haiti-play-for-peace, accessed 11 May 2021.
Pelé's Mysterious African Tour
Nascimento, Guilherme. Quote reproduced in 'Did Pelé cause fighting to cease during the Biafran War?' Africa Is a Country. https://africasacountry.com/2015/10/did-pele-by-playing-a-match-in-nigeria-cause-a-ceasefire-during-the-biafran-war, accessed 13 May 2021.
Pelé. Pelé: *The Autobiography* (London: Simon & Schuster UK, 2007).
The Lions Who Refused to Lose
Mahmoud, Younis. Quote reproduced in 'Iraq's Asian Cup win transcends sport.' Reuters. 30 July 2007. www.reuters.com/article/idINIndia-28728220070730, accessed 11 May 2021.
Vieira, Jorvan. Quote reproduced in 'Iraq united in football.' Al Jazeer. 13 July 2007. www.aljazeera.com/news/2007/7/13/iraq-united-in-football, accessed 11 May 2021.
Weird and Wonderful: Family vs Football
Bunyan, Nigel. 'Better Red than dead.' *Telegraph*, 28 November 2003. www.telegraph.co.uk/news/uknews/1447944/Better-Red-than-dead.html, accessed 11 May 2021.
The Greenest Football Team the World Has Ever Seen
Vince, Dale. Quote reproduced in 'Inside the world's first carbon neutral football club.' Diálogo Chino. 10 April 2020. https://dialogochino.net/en/climate-energy/34778-inside-forest-green-worlds-first-carbon-neutral-vegan-football-club/, accessed 11 May 2021.

Héctor Bellerín, the Footballer Who's Not Afraid to Branch Out
Bellerín, Héctor. Quote reproduced in '"It's a duty to do what we can with our platform".' Arsenal.com. www.arsenal.com/news/its-duty-do-what-we-can-our-platform, accessed 11 May 2021.

The Denmark Midfielder Determined to Make a Difference
Junge Pedersen, Sofie. Quote reproduced in 'Juventus' Sofie Junge Pedersen.' Green Sports Blog. 16 July 2020. https://greensportsblog.com/football4climate-juventus-sofie-junge-pedersen/, accessed 11 May 2021.

Creating Cool Kits Out of Ocean Waste
Gutsch, Cyrill. Quote reproduced in 'Plastic fantastic.' The *Sun*, 21 October 2018. www.thesun.co.uk/sport/football/7589580/parley-for-the-oceans-manchester-united/, accessed 11 May 2021.

'JJ', The Remarkable Referee Telling Girls to 'Play On!'
Roble, Jawahir. 'From Somalia to Wembley: The trailblazing referee told that football "is a man's game".' CNN. 2 September 2020. https://edition.cnn.com/2020/09/02/football/jawahir-roble-referee-uefa-cmd-spt-intl, accessed 11 May 2021.

Equal Playing Field: Football's Record Breakers
Murphy, Maggie. Quote reproduced in 'Equal Playing Field: Challenging the industry through world records.' Slowe. 1 June 2019. www.slowe.club/slowe/equal-playing-field-a-new-challenge, accessed 11 May 2021.

Welcome to the Street Child World Cup!
David, Dennis. Quote reproduced in 'Street children find hope in football.' FIFA.com. 19 March 2010. www.fifa.com/worldcup/news/street-children-find-hope-football-1183006, accessed 11 May 2021.

Hendra. Quote reproduced in 'Street Child World Cup Moscow 2018.' Street Child United. www.streetchildunited.org/our-sports-events/past-events/street-child-world-cup-moscow-2018/, accessed 11 May 2021.

The Supergoats Who Fell in Love with Football
Kumari, Radha. Quote taken from 'Sport for Good Award 2019: Yuwa.' Laureus. www.laureus.com/world-sports-awards/2019/sport-for-good/yuwa, accessed 11 May 2021.

Kumari, Neeta. Quote reproduced in 'Neeta's Story – Laureus girls' sports project in India.' Daimler. www.daimler.com/sustainability/corporate-citizenship/around-the-world/neeta-s-story.html, accessed 11 May 2021.

The Keepie-uppie Queen of COVID-19
Papworth-Heidel, Imogen. Quote reproduced in 'Coronavirus: Girl, 11, reaches 7.1m keepy-uppy target.' BBC.co.uk. November 2020. https://www.bbc.co.uk/news/uk-england-cambridgeshire-54810642, accessed 11 May 2021.

Alfie, the Humble Hero of Anfield
Fans Supporting Foodbanks. Twitter.com. 7 March 2018. https://twitter.com/sfoodbanks/status/971306608558043138, accessed 11 May 2021.

Robertson, Andrew. Letter reproduced on Twitter.com. 7 March 2018. https://twitter.com/__TR88/status/971461602305368065, accessed 11 May 2021.

The Brilliant Young Players Who Are Passing the Football On
Louis. Quote reproduced in 'Giving the Game.' US Soccer Foundation. https://ussoccerfoundation.org/success-stories/giving-the-game/, accessed 11 May 2021.